Author —

J-s. Trentman

PHILOSOPHY OF RELIGION SERIES

General Editor's Note

The philosophy of religion is one of several very active branches of philosophy today, and the present series is designed both to consolidate the gains of the past and to direct attention upon the problems of the future. Between them these volumes will cover every aspect of the subject, introducing it to the reader in the state in which it is today, including its open ends and growing points. Thus the series is designed to be used as a comprehensive textbook for students. But it is also offered as a contribution to present-day discussion; and each author will accordingly go beyond the scope of an introduction to formulate his own position in the light of contemporary debates.

JOHN HICK

Philosophy of Religion Series

General Editor: John Hick, H. G. Wood Professor of Theology,
University of Birmingham

Published

*John Hick (Birmingham University) Arguments
for the Existence of God
H. P. Owen (King's College, London) Concepts of Deity
Kai Nielsen (Calgary University)
Contemporary Critiques of Religion
Terence Penelhum (Calgary University)
Problems of Religious Knowledge
M. J. Charlesworth (Melbourne University)
Philosophy of Religion: The Historic Approaches
William A. Christian (Yale University) Oppositions of Religion Doctrines:
A Study in the Logic of Dialogue among Religions
Ninian Smart (Lancaster University) The Phenomenon of Religion
Hywel D. Lewis (King's College, London) The Self and Immortality*

Forthcoming titles

*Basil Mitchell (Oriel College, Oxford)
The Justification of Religious Belief
Nelson Pike (Californa University)
Religious Experience and Mysticism
Donald Evans (Toronto University) Religion and Morality
Dennis Nineham (Keble College, Oxford) Faith and History*

The Self and Immortality

HYWEL D. LEWIS

Professor of the History and Philosophy of Religion
King's College, University of London

MACMILLAN

AIF - 8419

© Hywel D. Lewis 1973

First published 1973 by
THE MACMILLAN PRESS LTD
London and Basingstoke
Associated companies in New York Dublin
Melbourne Johannesburg and Madras

SBN 333 02178 9

*Photoset and **Printed** in Great Britain by*
REDWOOD PRESS LIMITED
Trowbridge, Wiltshire

Contents

Preface

'The living know that they shall die.' Few will dispute this statement from the book of *Ecclesiastes*, at least where adult human beings are concerned. But what of Job's question? – 'If a man die shall he live again?' Here there will be more varied opinion. Most people down the ages have believed, at some level of their thoughts at least, that they will live again in some form. That belief has been deep in most forms of religion and culture. It has flagged, among reflective and sophisticated people, in the tough-minded agnosticism of our time. But interest in it has been much revived very recently, as a spate of books and articles show. It is hard to stop wondering whether there is more that we may expect than the limited span of our existence in this life. Sooner or later, most people, I suspect, find themselves deeply concerned about this question.

But we cannot go far with such a question without having to consider carefully how we are to think of ourselves as persons. On some views of what it is to be a person, future existence seems to be ruled out. On most views there are difficulties. It is with the question of how we are to think of ourselves as persons that this book is mainly concerned, but the question is examined in the context where we are asking also what is the prospect that we may live again in some form after we are dead.

The problems which present themselves here are varied, and I would have liked to have entered more deeply into some of them than has in fact been possible. Questions about memory, as will be evident, are central to my main theme. But I have not gone into them as fully as I would have liked. The reasons for that are two-fold. In the first place, the topic is a large one in itself and this volume already exceeds the normal length for books in this series.

Secondly, I hope to return to more extended discussion of memory in the more substantial book which I am preparing as the sequel to the first volume of my Gifford Lectures, *The Elusive Mind*. For similar reasons I have not gone carefully into the various forms of dualism of mind and body which interest me much in Oriental thought. Nor have I given the religious side of my topic the treatment which some readers may expect. I wrestle more with that in one of the volumes in preparation already mentioned.

For the present then I offer only an outline of what seem to me the main matters to be heeded regarding our status as creatures who may expect a destiny beyond our present existence.

I am much indebted to various persons who have helped in the final preparation of this book. Dr A. C. Ewing, who has himself made distinguished contributions to similar themes, read a nearly final version of the whole. Dr D.A. Rees, of Jesus College, Oxford, subjected the typescript to very careful scrutiny before it went to the printer. My gifted student, now starting academic work himself in the University of Birmingham, Mr J. J. Lipner, made the index and provided a detailed list of corrections to the proofs. Mr Keith Ward, of my own department of King's College, was also kind enough to read the proofs. I am deeply grateful to these gentlemen, but, as always, the responsibility for the form and substance of a book remains with the author.

I wish finally to thank the editor of this series, Professor John Hick, for encouraging me to write this book and for his patience and persistence in waiting while other projects were completed.

HYWEL D. LEWIS

1 Attitudes to Death

'Millions now living will never die.' This was the astonishing claim made by a large number of people not so long ago. Many of them, one must suppose, believed it – or was it perhaps the half-belief which Professor Price has been describing for us lately? They were certainly wrong, and if there is one thing about which all of us must be agreed, it is that we shall all die sooner or later. Indeed, we can be much more precise. Very few people live to be a hundred, and usually, when some do so, their faculties are so much impaired that they can do little to fend for themselves. In another twenty-five years a very large proportion of the adult population of the world will be dead. No one seriously doubts this although, on the face of it, no one seems to be seriously perturbed by it.

A purely formal doubt could, perhaps, be raised on the grounds that no empirical fact is absolutely certain or that there is no completely satisfactory way of establishing the principle of induction. Perhaps causal laws will suddenly cease to operate. But there is obviously very small comfort to be found here. No one throws away his alarm clock because he doubts, on some philosophical ground, that the dawn will break tomorrow. Philosophic doubt, whatever else it is, is not that kind of thing. And even if there should be some remote empirical doubt that things are not as certain as they seem, it is so remote in the case of the sun rising, as in the case of our approaching death, that no one in practice can do other than disregard it. We have no reason at all to doubt that we shall die, and that before many years are out.

One possibility, entertained as wishful thinking by those who sought blindly for some 'elixir of life' in the past and more scientifically today, is that the process of ageing which culminates in death may be arrested or reversed as we know more about the medical or biological facts or make new discoveries in biophysics. But at the moment the prospect of doing this is also very remote, although if it were accomplished it would make a radical change in the conditions of human existence and raise some very far-reaching questions. If the span of life could be extended, without serious impairment of our faculties, for how long should we do that? Would we wish to live for ever if we could? Some maintain that life would become intolerable if it were very much prolonged. Others do not think this quite so obvious. There is certainly much more that we could do if we lived longer. But even so, and allowing for vast extensions of our present powers, our lives would continue to be much circumscribed, and questions could still be raised about some more complete or abiding fulfilment of ourselves than is possible under the limitations of our temporal existence. In the meantime it is certain, for an indefinite future at least, that the span of life will remain substantially as it is at present. We shall all be dead before long.

I noted that this does not seem to perturb many people. We seem to take it in our stride. But there is also something curiously paradoxical about this attitude of mind. At another level, death has 'many terrors' for us. The thought of its approach is alarming, and if someone were to burst into the room brandishing a lethal weapon we would say that he had terrified the company, not merely because of the threat of acute physical pain, but, most of all, because he might have killed us. To kill people is 'a terrible thing'. The death penalty is often described as 'the supreme penalty' and one of the main objections to it is the extreme mental agony through which the sufferer will have passed as the days and hours and minutes run out – especially for a victim in the full pride and vigour of his youth. We deplore wars and other calamities because, among other things, they involve the slaughter of masses of people. There may be fates 'worse than death', but not many. Death is 'a terrible thing' and has been so represented in masque and play and story down the ages. We express our sympathy with the bereaved, not merely on account of their own loss and loneliness but because of the sad fate of their friend whose life is over. On the other hand, we talk of those who save life – doctors, rescue teams, relief workers – as engaged in noble work; and we are aghast when we learn that their efforts were in vain and that some great disaster has 'taken a terrible toll of human life'.

If life is so precious death cannot but be dreaded, and most people, I suspect, think that way if they are confronted with imminent death themselves. To know that you, like everyone else, are bound to die some day is one thing; it appears to be quite another to be faced with the stark reality within a short and measurable time. The reason for this may be a curious inability, woven, if one may so put it, in a cunning and kindly way into our nature, to envisage the passage of time in any realistic way. A year, in fact, passes very quickly, and yet when we are young a summer vacation seems like an eternity and growing up, though we know that it is somehow going on, so remote that we do not take it seriously – grown-ups are another species; and likewise, at later stages, our own envisionment of substantial slices of life enlarges them out of all proportion to our day-to-day sense of the passage of time, and as they grow old people seem again to live more and more in the present – and the past. The passage of time becomes 'notional' rather than 'real', in Newman's famous distinction.

This may account in part for the curious way in which we take our own mortality, as part of the general lot of mankind, so lightly, while also, in another vein, thinking of death as a dread and terrible eventuality. At the same time, it seems to be also not uncommon for many people to accept their own imminent death, once that has become certain to them, with surprising calm and fortitude. In some cases this is due to a deep religious faith. Men remain serene in the assurance of God's loving care or some similar vision of life by which death holds no dominion over them. But there have been plenty of examples also of death being faced with calmness and courage in the total absence of any religious faith. Socrates is a famous in-between example, for at times he appears as a model of a calm philosophical acceptance of whatever is in store, but as we all know he had a strong religious side to his thought and nature and, as presented in Plato's *Republic* for example[1], a belief in the indestructibility of the soul. David Hume is the classic example of the unperturbed sceptic and most of the readers of this book will have heard of Boswell's perplexed but good-natured taunting of Hume on his death-bed, eliciting nothing but an amused, one might almost say masterly, acceptance of his own certain annihilation.[2]

There have indeed been some who have expressed relief at having no reason to suppose that they will survive death. An outstanding example is the late C. D. Broad. Few have given the subject more thought than he, and he was immensely learned, not only in the explicit religious and philosophical literature of the subject, but also in less familiar byways of it, like psychical research (on which he was beyond doubt one of the greatest authorities of our time) and even necromancy. In the closing words of his notable *Lectures on Psychical Research* he wrote:

> To conclude, the position as I see it is this. In the known relevant *normal and abnormal* facts there is nothing to suggest, and much to counter-suggest, the possibility of any kind of persistence of the psychical aspect of a human being after the death of his body. On the other hand, there are many quite well attested *paranormal* phenomena which strongly suggest such persistence, and a few which strongly suggest the full-blown survival of a human personality. Most people manage to turn a blind eye to one or the other of these two relevant sets of data, but it is part of the business of a professional philosopher to try to envisage steadily both of them together. The result is naturally a state of hesitation and scepticism (in the correct, as opposed to the popular, sense of that word). I think I may say that for my part I should be slightly more annoyed than surprised if I should find myself in some sense persisting immediately after the death of my present body. One can only wait and see, or alternatively (which is no less likely) wait and not see.[3]

Professor H. H. Price, who is the most outstanding writer to be associated with Broad in these matters, but who takes a much more favourable and cheerful view of the prospects, on general religious grounds as well as in his study of psychical research, takes occasion also to warn us that there is a sombre side to the prospect of survival and that, in some respects, it may not be so much to be desired as we suppose. But I imagine that the attitude of most thinking persons today, so far as they turn their minds to the subject at all, is one of concern and dismay at the prospect of their own total eclipse, and there is evidence to suggest that, below the surface and at the levels which professional psychologists probe, there is much of the stark fear of death which motivated so much of the thought and activity of that most perceptive and forthright thinker and stylist, Thomas Hobbes.

A somewhat sombre poet of more recent times has written:

> But men at whiles are sober
> And think by fits and starts,
> And if they think, they fasten
> Their hands upon their hearts.

It was not just the thought of death which prompted the mood of sombre reflection in Housman's poems. There is much of unrequited love and other sorrows in them also. But the tragic view of death is never very far, subdued and sad rather than hysterical though sometimes bordering on the macabre; and this seems to me to reflect as well as anything the frame of mind of most normal persons as the inevitability of the end of their earthly days breaks into their consciousness, as it almost certainly does for all of us 'at whiles'.

In that mood the question which irresistibly frames itself is whether there is some prospect for us of more than our limited and swiftly passing time in this world. What does it mean to suppose that there is some 'life hereafter'? What reasons have we for thinking that this may actually happen? It is with these questions that the rest of this book will be concerned.

There are many ways in which it may be said that we live on after we are dead. It is said, for example, that the sort of immortality for which we should look, and by the thought of which we may be comforted, is that which we have when we live on in the memories of others and in our influence on their lives. Almost everyone can have some measure of immortality of this kind. We shall all be remembered somewhere for a while, not always perhaps with kindness. Our lives will also continue to have some influence. In the case of most of us this will be slight, although no doubt very precious for a time. It is nice to think we may be remembered with affection and tenderness by those who are themselves dear to us, and, to the extent that we have done good, it is comforting to think that this will continue to have some effect and be appreciated, notwithstanding the dismal view of Mark Antony that 'the evil that we do lives on' more obviously while the good 'is oft interred with our bones'. But for most people this comes largely to an end with the subsequent death of those who actually knew us, and G. E. Moore once suggested that all personal influence was neutralised after a hundred years or so, though it is hard to see how this could apply to notable people and how exactly the question is settled. Even the 'mute' and 'inglorious' may continue to have some very modest influence for an indefinite time; they are part of a related course of events. Those who have serious claims to fame may indeed find a great deal of satisfaction in this fact and especially in the thought that their achievements, most of all perhaps in art or literature or philosophy or science, live on and continue to be greatly enjoyed. The desire for fame of the right kind is not an ignoble one, provided it is kept in proper proportions and viewed realistically. The martyrs who 'lighted a candle' at the stake where they were burnt might not have been thinking of personal glory, though who would grudge it to them, but they would surely have been saddened to think that the candle would speedily splutter out. Doing something for posterity is a splendid aim, however little most of us can in fact accomplish, and no one should grudge for those who deserve it their proper place in 'the halls of fame'. The Scriptures invite us to praise famous men and sometimes set the model effectively themselves, as in *Hebrews XI*. The most solemn of Christian sacraments is one of remembrance. There is thus nothing improper or trivial in the consolation we may take in the thought that we should live on in this way when we are dead, although very few can aspire to a place among 'the immortals', as we speak of them.

But is this the sort of expectation men have when they console themselves, in the face of inevitable death for themselves or others, with the thought that 'this life is not all'? I do not think so. Comforting though it may be to think that you will be kindly remembered, we shall not ourselves participate in any way in this, at least not if death is the end. What the ordinary person wonders, when he talks of 'afterlife', is whether *he* will continue to exist in some way after his last breath is drawn in this world. What are the prospects for *him*? And can he hold out some hope that those whom he knew and loved and has 'lost awhile' are (or will be) alive all the same 'somewhere', and may even be restored to him some day? This hope may take crude forms or subtle forms, and we shall say more about that. But it is surely some personal hope of this kind (or fear in the case of some, like Broad) that makes people wonder whether this life is all, whether there is any hereafter, etc.; and they would presumably feel rather cheated if they were assured that of course there is life hereafter and death is not the end for any of us, only to learn that all that this amounts to is that they will at least have a trickle of influence after they are buried, and be tenderly remembered. Nor is this mainly because the immortality that most of us may expect in the latter sense is very sharply limited. It is not that most men realize that their claim to fame is slight or nonexistent, but that this is not the sort of thing they had in mind; and if someone were to mention, in casual conversation perhaps with a stranger, that he firmly believed in life after death and then it transpired that all he meant was that his life would germinate a little in the lives of others afterwards, the recipient of his confidence would feel cheated. The words would not be given their ordinary meaning, and if preachers speak from a Christian or any other pulpit of the 'hope of glory' and the 'resurrection of the dead' but intend this in no sense other than the continuing influence of our lives in the lives of others, it is a moot point whether they have not drifted far beyond the limits of proper adaptation and may not be in danger of a just accusation of prevarication or disingenuousness. This will have to be considered briefly later, but in the meantime it seems evident that the normal meaning of 'life hereafter', or its equivalents, is in terms of something that continues to be the case for the individual himself. It is *he* who will have been raised from the dead to 'live on in glory' however much this itself requires that the same destiny be in store for others to share it with him.

This goes also for those who contend that life eternal should be understood in the sense of some quality of the life we have here and now. It could well be that this submission contains an important truth. For many hold, as we shall see, that the life hereafter is certain to involve an essential transformation of ourselves and a special relationship to God. But it will normally be taken to mean more than that, namely that, however radically 'changed', we shall ourselves *be* in some form after our present life is ended. This is the essential claim and what the ordinary person would understand of us if we declared our belief in some kind of 'life hereafter'.

It will be noted that I have used the words 'beyond', 'after', 'again' and so on quite freely and without qualification. It could well turn out, however, that no terms of this kind are entirely adequate. This is because there is a difficult problem about the sense in which after-life will have the sort of temporal quality to which we are accustomed now. When we speak of God as eternal we usually think of him as not being in time at all or being beyond time. It is not possible for us to form a clear conception, and on some views we have no conception at all, of what it would be to exist in a timeless way. But it is also held that this is no bar to our thinking that God must exist in some such way, for God, it is maintained, is transcendent and beyond the grasp of our thought in any explicit way. On the other hand, others maintain that, while we must think of the eternity of God in this fashion, it does not follow that life eternal for us as finite beings, however much it may involve a peculiarly close relationship to God, can be understood in a way that does not involve some kind of sequence. This is one of the difficult questions to which it may be impossible for us in our present existence to have a proper answer. But in the meantime we should not be deterred by such considerations from giving some substantial content to the idea of a life hereafter. For if anyone is to affirm this at all, in any way related to our normal understanding of these terms, it must be in the sense of our continuing to be in some fashion to which we can only refer in temporal terms like 'after', 'again', etc. Even if these terms are misleading, and if the 'life eternal' that is to interest us means a good deal more than just being alive again, it is even more misleading to dispense with them altogether.

The notion that it is futile to suppose that we shall actually live again after we are dead but that, in the light of this, we must continue to use the language of after-life or resurrection for certain religious purposes and interpret it in a new way, will need to be considered in due course. But in the meantime we start at least with the idea that, notwithstanding obvious difficulties, the idea of a life hereafter or of immortality is normally understood in terms of our existence not being finally ended with our death.

But in that case the question which first arises is the question what do we mean by the self or person, the *me*, which is expected to survive. Perhaps we shall find that, when we think of what we really are, it becomes at once impossible to suppose that we can in any sense survive the dissolution of our bodies at death. Even if we are not led to this conclusion, the way we think of ourselves could, nonetheless, much affect the form in which we understand our possible survival and the strength of any considerations adduced in support of the view that we do in fact survive. It seems plain, therefore, that we must begin with the question of the nature of persons and their identity.

2 Mind and Body

When we turn to the question of what it is for us to be the persons we are, there seem to be two things to say about it at once. It is plain that, in life as we know it now at least, we have bodies, and it seems also clear that we are in some way more than our bodies, that we have minds as well. This is how we would put it for rough and ready purposes. But what does it mean to say that we *have* a mind, or for that matter, that we *have* a body? When we speak of having something we usually think of some entity which, as we say, belongs to us. But there is also a looser use of the verb 'to have' in these contexts, as when we say that we 'have' a pain. If we say that we 'have a mind' are we referring to some kind of entity, and in what sense would we say that this entity belongs to us? And is the body an entity, and in what way does it belong to us? Are we composite beings, having both mind and body in some relation to one another? If so, is one part or the other dispensable, and what, in any case, is the relation between them?

The moment these questions are raised there appears to be an air of artificiality about them, and philosophers of today have not been slow to point this out. It would be odd to think of myself having a mind in some way like having a typewriter which I carry around with me to use as required; and it seems no less odd to think of my body in the same way. It seems more natural, in some ways at least, to say that I am myself without drawing too rigid a distinction between my mind and my body. I am writing on this page now. Mind and body, we might say, are inseparably involved, they are not two things that we carry about with us like entities in the world around us. They are ourselves. All the same we also draw a sharp distinction between mind and body, not merely when we say that the spirit is willing and the flesh is weak, referring to conflicting strains within the same person, but in more explicit philosophical reflection. For clearly there is more going on in my present activity than the posture of my body and the movements of my hands guiding the pen over the page. I intend and understand what is said. I convey my thoughts to paper, as we put it; and my thoughts do not seem to be the same kind of thing as the states and movements of my body. We speak metaphorically of their being 'within me' and so on. But this is clearly metaphor. My thoughts are not to be located anywhere in my body. You do not find them by cutting me up or taking an X-ray. But they also seem real enough. Indeed, it is my thoughts that I really wish to convey to you, and I shall do so in a form in which this pen and paper will not be directly involved at all. You will read the printed page, and for all you know, and for all that matters, I might have dictated it all. It seems very difficult thus to avoid drawing some distinction between mind and body, and perhaps the mistake is to think of the distinction too much on the lines of a distinction between two connected things in the external world. On the other hand, if we are over subtle and draw the distinction solely in terms of different conceptions of our over-all activities, we may find ourselves doing less than justice to our fairly clear impression that some quite radical distinction requires to be drawn between mind and body.

Perhaps our best course will be to start with the notion that a quite radical distinction has to be drawn between mind and body, especially as we are considering the question in the context of an enquiry into the possibility of our surviving the so-called death of the body. We can thus see whether the distinction can be drawn without the crudities which have occasioned the understandable misgivings of recent philosophers, who are so well aware that we do not normally think of ourselves as a conjunction of separate parts on a strict analogy with some composite physical thing. How then shall we think of mind and of mental processes? Are these themselves in any sense physical? It will be best to consider this question in a general way to start, and defer consideration of the sense in which we may also wish to distinguish between the mind and its own processes.

The view that our minds are altogether different in nature from our bodies has been maintained by some of the most notable thinkers of the past. They include Plato, Augustine, Descartes, and Kant (cf. below, pp. 33–7). The person whose name is most closely associated with this view of persons in recent critical discussion is Descartes, but the contribution of Kant to our understanding today of the way we ought to think of a self which is not a bodily existent, is considerable, difficult though his position is in some ways. The reasons for the prominence given, by friend and foe alike, to Descartes are two-fold. In the first place, he provides an extremely forthright statement of the position which, in some moods at least, is that of the ordinary person. In the second place, he is the one who has committed most obviously the mistakes to which, according to very influential thinkers, we are particularly liable when we try to draw too sharp a distinction between mind and body. It will be well, therefore, to begin with Descartes. The usual label for the position he holds is 'dualism'. This term is also used in other contexts, for instance in discussing the relation between the world and God. I shall use it for the sort of view of the relation between mind and body which we find in the work of the thinkers listed above and especially of Descartes. What then was Descartes' view?

Descartes held that the mind was a thing – *res* or substance. Body is also a thing. It is characteristic of a thing that it exists by itself alone. This did not mean for Descartes that finite things did not have to be created and sustained in being. He thought they were so created by God. Some of his successors understood his account of thinghood in such a way that there could only be one thing, namely God; and this led to the view that we all had to be regarded, along with everything else in the world around us, as modes, elements or limitations of the being of God himself. Descartes did not hold that view. He thought that finite beings were quite distinct from the being of God and from one another. What he really meant when he said that a thing must exist by itself alone was that we can form a clear conception of it without going beyond what we take it to be in itself, although we can learn of certain relations in which it also stands to other things. The latter are in no way essential to the thing in question. There are, according to Descartes, many physical things of this kind. The essence of them, according to him, is to be extended. This runs into grave difficulties at once. We think of physical things as having colour, smell, weight, etc. What would a tomato be if it had none of these? Descartes' answer is somewhat ambiguous. He seems never quite certain where to place things like colours, sounds and smells. For he will not have it that they are part of the mind. They are due to the states of physical bodies and yet not properly belonging to them. This ambiguity was never properly resolved by Descartes. In addition, if we hold that the essence of a thing is to be extended, it is hard to see how exactly its boundaries are to be defined, and this is indeed a difficulty which presents itself, in our thought about physical things, quite independently of taking them in quite such an abstract way as their mere extendedness. Is there perhaps something arbitrary in the way we parcel things off in the external world? Is it some rough and ready division we have for certain purposes? A table is many pieces of wood, and they can be divided again *ad infinitum*. Some important thinkers have certainly held this view, not only of material things but of everything. Descartes, however, held that the universe contained a number of entities whose independence or distinctness was no arbitrary matter. I shall not dwell on the difficulties of this view as it affects material things. Nor will I go into the question how the extendedness of anything can be understood without thinking of space as in some way more or other than the actual extendedness of any particular thing, however large. For we have to limit ourselves if we are not to find ourselves trying to deal with more fundamental questions than can be adequately considered within the compass of one small book. We all know roughly what we mean by the particular things in the world around us – books, trees, mountains and so on; and we know that there are causal relations between those, however difficult it may be to understand the idea of causality when we think hard about it. We know also that one such physical thing is one's own body. Descartes holds that a mind is a similar entity which stands in a special relation to one material entity, namely one's own body.

The essence of mind, according to Descartes, is thought. A mind is a 'thinking thing'. This also presents a difficulty at once, and that has been the source of some of the most persistent misgivings people have had about a Cartesian view of mind and body. For we have to ask: What is meant here by 'thinking'? Descartes understands this in a fairly broad sense to include imagination and feelings as well as doubting, understanding, etc., but the distinctive thing about us as conscious creatures, all the same, is the ability to reason. We distinguish sharply, perhaps too sharply, between ourselves and other creatures by claiming the possession of reason; and the model of what it is to reason is argument or proof of the kind we find in geometry, for instance. Descartes, moreover, began his philosophical thinking with a special concern about certainty. It seems possible to doubt so many things. Is there something we cannot doubt at all, and how far then can we extend this certainty? Could we, for instance, know anything about God in this fool-proof way? It would, on the face of it at least, be excellent if we could. We need have no worries on this score any more; and all sensible people would have to agree. For we would have a wholly dependable method. The difficulty, or at least one main one, is that in geometry and arithmetic we do not seem to establish the existence of anything or any other matter of fact. Descartes, however, remained unperturbed. He was determined to prove the main things in philosophy by the sort of reasoning we find in mathematics, and this, as he understood it, meant starting with certain ideas which were simple in the sense that we could not break them up further, but which we saw (or intuited) to be sound or valid, and then combining them in ways which we also saw to be the appropriate ones. This, in its simplest terms, is Descartes' famous method, and he thought he could use it to prove, among other things, the existence of God. But what he started with was his own existence, and what he himself thought he was committed

to in his famous 'I think, therefore I am', was a being whose
essential activity was that of reasoning in the way indicated.
To reason in this way was the important thing about us. It
is for these reasons that Descartes is thought to be an outstanding example of a rationalist.

It is well to add that, in many of these matters, the position of Descartes has a great deal in common with that of
Plato. He also was an outstanding believer in the power of
pure reason, and he showed a great contempt at times for
those who suppose that we can learn anything of importance by looking at the world or interpreting things. We just
think things out and see what must be true in this way,
although the process culminates in a vision of some
supreme Good which affords us the key to everything else
that may perplex us. The soul is not itself a part of the
system of truth which our reason apprehends in this way,
and it has other components than reason, namely spirit (a
principle of activity or energy) and appetite. But appetite is
to be severely controlled, and the function of spirit is to side
with reason. Physical appetite is not evil, but it can easily
become a nuisance (if over-indulged and also if quite frus-
trated) and our aim should be, most of all if we show some
flair for things of the mind, to live an ascetic life and curb
our physical appetites in order to help the powers of the
mind to their full flowering in the discernment of inter-
related rational truths. The pursuit of such an aim requires
physical fitness, and Plato lays great stress on this[1] as well
as upon a clean and healthy physical environment condu-
cive to the best exercise of the powers of the mind. It is important also for the good man to take his responsible share
in running his community. He is not a recluse, and he is far
from the ascetic who neglects or tortures his body. Fitness,
health and pleasant surroundings do indeed matter, as
does the society of those of like mind and gifts to ourselves.
The good life, as Plato thought of it, was certainly not a
dull or restricted one. All the same the body plays a very
subordinate part, and it is regrettable that we have any
need of it. The more we draw the powers of the mind
upwards from earth the better, and what this means above
all is that the powers of the mind in grasping the truths

that are rationally necessary and eternal should be given the fullest play. The body could drop out of the picture were it not that at present it could make itself a nuisance. Some day we shall be rid of it and its inhibiting demands – and what a change that will be. As Plato puts it in a famous passage:

> Well then, that the soul is immortal is established beyond doubt by our recent argument and the other proofs; but to understand her real nature, we must look at her, not as we see her now, marred by association with the body and other evils, but when she has regained that pure condition which the eye of reason can discern; you will then find her to be a far lovelier thing and will distinguish more clearly justice and injustice and all the qualities we have discussed. Our description of the soul is true of her present appearance; but we have seen her afflicted by countless evils, like the sea-god Glaucus, whose original form can hardly be discerned, because parts of his body have been broken off or crushed and altogether marred by the waves, and the clinging overgrowth of weed and rock and shell has made him more like some monster than his natural self. But we must rather fix our eyes, Glaucon, on her love of wisdom and note how she seeks to apprehend and hold converse with the divine, immortal, and everlasting world to which she is akin and what she would become if her affections were entirely set on following the impulse that would lift her out of the sea in which she is now sunken, and disencumber her of all that wild profusion of rock and shell, whose earthy substance has evacuated her, because she seeks what men call happiness by making earth her food. Then one might see her true nature, whatever it may be, whether manifold or simple[2].

This is in many ways a splendid vision. But it gives us, not merely Plato's sense that it will be well to have our present limitations and ills removed, but also that there is little, if any, positive worth in anything that we associate with the body. We just happen to be encased in it now and must come to terms with that. There are close analogues to this in some idealistic movements of today, for example, among some followers of Sri Aurobindo in India, who set out to establish a city and community very like Plato's ideal of every man giving his best in an environment designed to bring out the best in us, but in an impersonal way where close attachment and involvement in the passing show of this world on its own account has no high place. There are metaphysical and religious aspects of this aspiration in India which we do not find in Plato and we shall note them later. But for the moment I wish only to note a further example of a tendency to elevate the powers of the mind in a way that makes little of bodily attainments in themselves.

In the case of Plato, as has often been pointed out, the fault lies mainly in the too rigid separation of appetite and reason. Appetite tends to remain brute appetite, as if nothing distinguished us at this level from brutes besides our ability, through the exercise of reason, to find a safer and more lasting satisfaction of our needs and desires. But reason permeates and transforms our so-called physical pleasures; eating is not just a matter of keeping body and soul together and giving us pleasant tastes. The hedonist who sets out to savour his pleasures in that way too deliberately is apt, as in the well-known paradox of hedonism, to defeat himself and be bored. 'The sauce to meat is ceremony', and many things besides. A physical caress is not just a means to an agreeable sensation; and the love and regard we have for one another are not for abstract qualities of mind but for what each one is in the warmth and liveliness of his own person in his wholeness, not as an embodiment of some abstract quality or virtue. Even the physical enjoyment that brutes have, the bird on the wing or feeding its young or trilling in the sky, may have more to it in reality, and not just in romantic notions of our own, than we usually think of as the mere satisfaction of physical urge or appetite. We have learnt to credit the higher animals with a great deal which they share with us, including sensitivity and response to affection. It seems thus to be a great mistake, and it was a very serious one for Plato and some other notable thinkers, to isolate the so-called physical side of our nature too completely from the rational one.

Our more specifically mental activities derive much of their colour and importance from material and particular factors that we take up into them.

It was for reasons of this kind that Archbishop William Temple became so severe a critic of Descartes,[3] who was likewise thought to have wrapped himself up too much in an intellectual world of his own. This was 'the Cartesian *faux-pas*' and it led us into a tunnel far from 'the daylight of common-sense'. We shall meet the complaint again in other forms. How far precisely, in the form we have just been noting, the complaint can be made to stick with Descartes is not altogether clear. He was certainly not led to any severely ascetic conception of life or to any harsh denunciation of material enjoyment. His own constitution was not strong, and he liked to work in comfort – usually in bed with the window wide open. He took a great interest in what was known in his day about the way our bodies function and he himself gave much impetus to the studies which prepared the way for modern medicine. He took great interest in medical problems – as his detractors would do well to remember. He was also much at the mercy of the sort of picture of the physical world which was common among scientists and philosophers in his day. This tended to present the world of nature, including the activities of brutes, as one vast mechanism in which everything happened by simple propulsion of one thing by another. It is not surprising, in this situation, that someone who affirmed the distinctness of mind should have conceived the opposition in a way that presented the mind almost wholly in terms of severely intellectual operations. A merely 'thinking thing' might thus appear to lack a great deal that we normally consider essential for personal existence, though how far Descartes himself intended this and was truly at fault is another matter.

What matters for us is that, whatever may have been the mistakes of Descartes and of Plato before him, a correction is not very difficult to make. We have only to include, within our notion of 'a thinking thing', the mental activities which Descartes, in his preoccupation with our more severely intellectual operations, left out. To the mind will thus

belong perceptual awareness of the world around us, emotional reactions and aspirations of various kinds, discern-
ments of worth in arts or morals, loves or hates and other
personal concerns, moral choice (anticipated at least by
Descartes himself in his account of 'the liberty of indiffer-
ence'), together with so-called physical sensations like pain
and somatic sensations 'within' our bodies. The latter, together with perceptual experience, might be thought to be
doubtful starters for the status of strictly mental reality. For
the body seems to be peculiarly involved in our attainment
of them. Pain, or what we usually know as physical pain, is
'in' some part of the body; and what would touch or smell
be like without the body? At the same time there seems to
be a case for saying that, even if the body is involved in
more than normal causal dependence in these cases, the experiences themselves are, *qua* experiences, mental; it would
certainly be hard to give an account of them entirely in physical terms. Perhaps the issue can be left open for the present and we can remain content with noting that there
appears to be no immediate objection to extending Descartes' notion of what 'a thinking thing' might include. Perhaps we could say instead 'a thing that has experience'.

One observation is required here, however, if we are to
avoid misunderstanding at the start in including perceptual
awareness among the constituents, as it were, of mental
being as we find it. For the view is sometimes held that what
we normally describe as the external world is itself dependent on being perceived by us. This is what was involved in
the form of idealism defended by Berkeley. It could then be
argued, and has been so argued recently by Keith Campbell in his *Body and Mind*, p.8, that on this view, there is no
problem of what is mental and what is not, and thus no
problem of the relation of mind to body or matter. For
matter has been eliminated. But this would at least be a
very serious misunderstanding of Berkeley himself. For he
would certainly not say that all presentations of sense are
themselves mental. A colour, for instance, is not itself a disposition or mode of the mind, although it is certainly mind-
dependent. It cannot exist except as perceived, apart from
some way, unknown to us, in which it must exist in the

mind of God. But it is not itself part of the mind or experience. The perceiving is the mental factor, and this implies
something not mental, albeit mind-dependent, which is
perceived. We have, in the terms of a later writer, Samuel
Alexander, to distinguish between experienc*ing* and the experienc*ed*, the enjoyment, in Alexander's terms again, and
that which is enjoyed. There would thus remain a problem,
even if its terms were altered, of the relation between the
properly mental component in perceptual and other experience and the natural order as we perceive it, whatever its
ultimate status. It is not in fact clear that the main problem
of the relation of mind and body would be affected at all
directly by the adoption of a Berkeleyan view.

To return, we have now the view that the mind is a thing
which has certain states and operations of an entirely
mental kind but in no way restricted to rarefied ratiocina-
tion. What else would Descartes say about it? He would say
that the mental thing, in our own cases, though not, of
course, in the case of God, was conditioned by physical
things whose nature, *qua* physical, was radically different
from mind. Physical things acted, not only on one another
but also on mind, though invariably through one body
which each one of us calls his own body. The mind in turn
affects this particular body and thereby other bodies in the
world of nature. The term which best describes this is
'interaction', and so the view which we have is that minds
and bodies are of a radically different nature but that they
interact. This must be contrasted with the position adopted
by some of Descartes' immediate followers, who held that
minds and bodies did not strictly influence one another but
that things had been so arranged, or in some way come
about, that there was a neat and exact dove-tailing of certain mental and physical processes which made it look as
though they affected one another, although in fact they fol-
lowed without deviation the course prescribed by laws or
other conditions appertaining solely to their own natures.
There would thus be complete physical determinism in the
external world, although it would look as though the movement of my pen on this paper, for example, had come about
through my having certain thoughts and intending that

movement. It is a fortunate accident, as far as my own thoughts and my body are concerned at least, that these are so happily conjoined. The name for this theory is psycho-physical parallelism, and there are various versions of it and explanations of how, on a more final account, things come about in this way – the Occasionalists, for example, holding that God had so arranged it. Others maintained that, while mental processes had some kind of shadowy reality distinct from material processes, they were in fact determined throughout or produced by material events, including in particular changes in our own bodies, which accounted for our seeming to effect certain changes through our inten-tions. This was called epiphenomenalism, and it had many supporters in Descartes' day. He himself resisted the temp-tation to think in these terms, strong though it was in the materialistic climate of much of the scientific and philo-sophical thought of his time. He made some concessions which he need not have made to the ideas about the exter-nal world which prevailed in his day, but he also held firmly that the state of our minds, or our mental processes, did make a difference in some ways to what would otherwise have happened in the physical world. The mind influenced the body and the body in turn influenced the mind.

I must now add that this seems to me in essentials a very sound view, although we shall have to modify Descartes' way of putting it in some ways later – or at least rid our-selves of ideas that are associated with Descartes' view. But it is, in some regards at least, at odds with the way we com-monly think of ourselves. We do not normally picture our-selves as in some way attached to our bodies, or of our bodies as linked to us and manipulated by us like some other item of the world around us. The relation, if that is what it is, is a peculiarly intimate one; and indeed, in our ordinary thoughts and behaviour, we do not stop to draw a distinction between ourselves and our bodies. We think of ourselves as just being our bodies, or at least of being our-selves in a way in which our own bodies are essentially involved. I am now sitting at this table, my fingers write these words on the page – this is me, I am here. I do not sit inside my body like a driver in a taxi (or, in Descartes' own comparison, often forgotten by his detractors, 'like a pilot in a vessel')[4]. It is *I* who move around the room and open the window, *I* am in the house and not in the garden; it is not some shadow of me that sits in the chair, it is me, myself. My wife is the one standing at the corner of the room looking out at the garden. Soon she will go down and call me to join her for lunch. I shall not think of her voice as a bell she is sounding – *she* will call, and she will sit at one side of the table, I on the other. *We* shall be lifting our knives and forks, not some robots we are controlling; and if I slip and cut my finger it will be my finger that will hurt, not some remote controller to which all is relayed. If I turn pale at the sight of blood, it is *I* who pale; and if my wife smiles sweetly to overcome such childishness of mine, it is *she* who smiles. She just does not turn it on, she smiles.

I have gone on at some length in this vein because it is very important to get the strength and the feel of the point I have just been making. For it is out of this kind of thinking and talking most of all that the main opposition and criticism of a Cartesian position draws its strength, especially today. It is also by understanding where the plausibility of such criticism lies, and by taking the full force of the sort of reactions I have just been depicting, that we can understand properly the way to think of ourselves and our bodies – and also in fact of our relations with one another. But it seems clear that there is at least something inadequate, most of all for detached reflection, in the picture of oneself which I have just been presenting.

For when all has been said in that vein, it remains clearly the case that more is involved, in my being in this chair now, than my body being just propped up in the chair; I am sitting in the chair, and what does this mean? Moreover, I have been active, and this means more than that my fingers have in fact moved the pen across the page; I have been intending all this, and I could have stopped it at any time. The movement of the pen has been, furthermore, to put certain thoughts on paper. But I do not literally put anything on the paper besides ink. I have been thinking while writing and following out a certain train of thoughts which has been dominant in deciding what I have been doing. If I get stuck in my thinking or in my choice of words, I stop writing. There appears, therefore, to have been some process of thinking, some course of my thoughts as we say, going on at the same time as my overt behaviour and the state of my body. I have been puzzling things out and also 'guiding' the pen and maintaining my purpose to sit at my table. What are these thoughts and intentions? They clearly do not go on in me in the sense that you might find them if you cut open my body or exposed me to some powerful X-ray. But they seem equally real and important in the full story of what I have been doing.

My thoughts, in short, are not visible or tangible; they have no location. It is not simply that they are not in my body, they are not anywhere; they have no extension. My thoughts about Descartes' teaching have neither length nor breadth, they have no weight or colour, except in a purely metaphorical sense. It would be absurd to ask how long or how blue they were, though one could quite properly ask how long was I thinking them – when did I start thinking about Descartes and when did I turn my attention to something else, how intermittent have my thoughts been, to what other matters, the sight of the trees from my window, the droning of a plane, have I given attention? It would not be easy in practice to answer the latter questions, at any rate with any precision. I could say, as a rough and ready answer, that I have been thinking about the mind–body problem fairly continuously for the last hour, but I have been doing much besides, including taking sips of tea from a cup. How to record and measure the changes and continuities in our thoughts with precision is a difficult question, and the best person to cope with it is the psychologist and anyone who might help him to invent the appropriate techniques. But the difficulties here are mainly practical, not logical, except perhaps for deciding what counts as a continuous course of thought when there are always some changes. But there is no inherent absurdity in asking how long I have been thinking about Descartes' problems this morning – or in bed last night. Indeed we do speak just like that – 'I thought about it for a long time last night'. The only difficulty is that of getting greater precision. Our thoughts do take time for us to think them – they are, as we say, 'in time'; and it is certainly difficult, in spite of what some mystics and others say, for most of us at least to form the slightest idea of what it would be like to have any kind of experience that did not take time. But if our thoughts are 'in time', essentially and unavoidably so perhaps, they seem equally certainly not to be in space. They have no length or breadth.

It may be thought that, if this extends to myself as a being having these thoughts – and we shall return to that question shortly – I might be landed with the seeming absurdity of denying that I was in this room now. This objection has in fact been put to me from time to time – 'Come off it', my interlocutor would say, 'stop being clever, you know quite well where you are, you are sitting in your chair in this room'. Well, yes, certainly in a sense. If I denied in a court of law that I was in this room this morning I would commit perjury. I am clearly here, and that is what my wife would say if someone asked for me. But what does this mean? It means that my body is in this room with all the results of that for what I have been doing and undergo-ing – I would have had very different thoughts on the tennis court. But my thoughts are not here. That is not because they, or I who am having them, are somewhere else. The absurdity in saying that I am not in this room would only arise if it meant that I was somewhere else – in London or Paris or America or the moon. I have no means of being physically in two places at once, or at least if I have it would take us quite a while to tease out what exactly this would mean – in terms of clairvoyance, perhaps, or causation at a distance, or (could it be, as some claim?) inhabiting two bodies, or more (see Chapter 6). But the point at the moment is that, whatever else may be said about my loca-tion, there is no sense in which my thoughts or other mental processes are themselves extended. They are not the kind of things which can occupy space. At the same time they are real enough, they do occur, although some writers today, as we shall see, question this way of putting it.

This is what Socrates, as Plato describes him, had in mind long ago when he playfully teased his grieving friends

a short while before his execution. Crito wished to know
how they should bury him.

> 'In any way you like', he replied, 'only you must get hold
> of me, and take care that I do not walk away from you.'
> Then he turned to us, and added with a smile, 'I cannot
> make Crito believe that I am the same Socrates who has
> been talking and conducting the argument; he fancies
> that I am the other Socrates whom he will soon see, a
> dead body – and he asks, How shall he bury me?'[5]

But once we revert quite firmly to this way of talking –
and it seems quite impossible to avoid doing so – we are
back with the nagging feeling which I also tried to convey
very forcibly a little while back, namely that it is somehow
highly artificial to speak, as Socrates does, of our being
quite apart from our bodies – 'the other Socrates', as if
there were two of us – rather than being ourselves truly the
persons whom other people see or touch or fondle or take
around in cars or assault. If you assault me it is not like
damaging my car, you injure me; if I am kissed on the lips,
I am kissed, not a phantom or some appurtenance of mine.
How do we cope with this dilemma?

Some will say at this point that the dilemma is just what
philosophers invariably end up in by tackling their problems in the present way. There must be something phoney
about an investigation where we seem to be driven round
in circles saying now one thing and then, with equal conviction, the opposite. We have, perhaps, a pseudo problem
on our hands and the whole enterprise must be radically
changed before we make any headway. We must in fact see
that it is pointless to ask the kind of question I have been
asking, and some will go on to maintain that the root
trouble lies in certain ways in which we talk, or in a radical
misunderstanding of the function of language. Once all this
is corrected we shall turn our minds to something else
(though it is not altogether clear to what) and stop trying
desperately to say that we are our bodies and that quite
clearly we are not.

This approach to the subject, a philosophical defeatism
it seems to me, will be met and commented upon more

directly in a moment. For in one way or another it covers
some of the most important and influential discussions of
the subject in recent times. But for the moment I must ask
my reader to consider seriously whether I have been playing some kind of trick upon him or am subject to some radical confusion myself. I have indeed been saying things like –
'We *talk* of ourselves being this and that', or 'We say that
we', etc., and all this means is that this is how we think or
what we believe; and I must ask the reader to ask himself –
irrespective of the particular terms in which the points are
put, and of some modifications in the precise way they are
presented – does he not find himself forced to think in these
ways himself if he turns his mind seriously to the problem?
Is not this just one of the truly exciting things about philosophy that it leads us to some impasse, like the present one,
in the process of resolutely trying to *think* as hard and clearly as we can about the way things appear unmistakably to
be, about what we seem forced to recognise, but with the
firm implication in consequence that some solution there
clearly must be and that renewed endeavour of further
thinking, raised upon and not despising what we have
already thought, may put us in the way of finding it? Perhaps what we need, to make progress in our task, is to be a
little more subtle in some respects than we have managed to
be as yet.

To this end I would like again to refer to the course of
philosophical thinking about our problem in the past. For it
often happens in philosophy that the dead-end at which we
seem to arrive along one way of thinking has the way out of
it opened for us in examination of some quite radically different approach to the subject and the difficulties, equally
insuperable it seems, that present themselves along that
course as well. We are not first in the field, or the first to be
baffled; and, while we may not find a ready-made solution
we can take over *in toto* in some particular work of the past,
we may find the way forward in the swing of opinion from
one side to the other among those who have struggled
before us. This does not give us a rigid and formal dialectic
of thought which will itself, once we get the trick of it, do
the work for us like a computer, but it does give us the more

exciting and creative dialectic of live and effortful thinking.

3 The Pure Self

The first point to be noted at this stage is that, soon after Descartes and his followers set out to establish what must be true about ourselves and the world around us by just thinking out hard what must in fact be the case, taking mathematics, understandably but foolishly, as the only model for the proper way to arrive at the truth, a group of British thinkers, starting mainly with Locke, took almost the opposite course, in this case also taking their cue from science, and insisted that, if we wish to get at the truth, we must rely solely on what the brute facts of our actual experience force upon us; we must have recourse to experiment and observation, in short to looking. This meant that the immediate items of any knowledge that we have of the world around us must be the colours, smells, sounds, etc. that we strictly experience. These come to us through our five senses, but this adds nothing beyond the fact that we do have these distinctive experiences under certain bodily conditions, with our eyes open in a certain direction, etc. But all the same they do seem to 'come' in some way – they are 'presented'; and Locke concluded that they came or emanated from entities which had some of the properties of sounds and sights, such as shape and location, but of which we could form no other notion beyond the fact that they must have the properties which cause us, in certain conditions, to have the experiences themselves. He did add, however, that the properties of which we learn in this indirect way must belong to or 'inhere' in distinct things or 'substances'. But as the thing and its properties are not directly inspectible, but rather quite behind the scenes as it were, we can know nothing properly about it beyond the fact that it must somehow *be* as the thing to which particular properties belong – 'a something we know not what'.

In these last ideas, however, Locke appears to have gone a good deal further than looking. We do not see or touch these entities or things as they really are in themselves, they are things we are 'to suppose', in Locke's own words. Nor was it long before this apparent inconsistency of policy was pointed out – we seemed to have gone a long way beyond the original 'way of ideas', sticking firmly to just what our senses report. The main name here, to continue a familiar story for a moment, is that of Berkeley, and he maintained that, if we had no conception of what the mysterious entities behind the scene could be, we had no warrant even to affirm their existence, least of all on a proper empiricist policy of building up our knowledge out of sense experience. We could dispense with the alleged material substances, and this drastic operation could leave us then with just the world of sights and sounds, etc. as these actually happen. These could not happen, it was also argued, except as someone has the experience. On the other hand, we are not the authors of them ourselves, nor do *we* guarantee the regularity and system with which they happen which makes the experience we have an ordered dependable one in which we can live and manipulate things and adjust our actions sensibly to what is likely to happen. But if the idea of some totally mysterious second world does not help to provide the explanations we seem to need here, we can find our clue perhaps in the way sounds and smells and sights seem to depend on our having them. If our own having of these, in ways we cannot avoid, given the conditions, calls for some further accounting, the answer could most plausibly be found in some way in which they are also present to some mind superior to ours; and Berkeley was led in this way to think of God as the ultimate author of the world of nature directly implanting the sensations that we have in our minds. The adequacy of this procedure need not hold us up now. It must suffice to note, in very rough outline, how the supposed independent material world drops out in Berkeley's celebrated immaterialism. Berkeley did not, however, think of the world of our senses as just modes of our minds. It is a world we apprehend or perceive, though it exists in being perceived. We know the mind that perceives in a radically different way through 'notions', though there is hardly anything we can say about 'notions' beyond our recognition that we do know minds in this way.

It is here that we must refer to the third person in the famous trio of British empiricists, namely Hume. He held on the one hand, that we could not fail to believe in an independent material world but that, on the other, we could provide no justification for this belief, any more than we could, by either reason or experience, justify the confidence we have in the patterns or seemingly causal linkages of the various ingredients of our experience which remain thus, it would seem, in the last resort fortuitous. We come to have certain strong expectations due to the way things happen; and the contiguities, in time and space, of the elements of our experience enable us to group them and identify things as things. But there is no necessity here, or if at all a psychological one and not something in the nature of things, beyond the passing scene as it comes. This is how the empiricist 'way of ideas' should be worked out, according to Hume, to its logical conclusion. But he went a great deal further, in determined clear-sighted pursuance of the same policy. He turned the same criticism against the idea of the perceiving mind which we know through notions. Notions, whatever else they are, are not looking. We cannot turn round from our contemplation of the outward scene and look at or observe ourselves looking at it. If we try to do that we find there is nothing to look at. One can of course note what sort of, experiences we do have and how they affect one another. We can observe ourselves in this way, but that is a very different matter from observing or contemplating ourselves engaged in observing the outward scene; and plainly, if it is a matter of looking in any sense like the way we look at a table or a landscape, Hume is right. We catch no glimpse of ourselves in this way. There is just nothing to glimpse, not because we have not learnt the trick of it or not invented the proper technique, but because the undertaking is inevitably doomed to failure; and the conclusion which Hume drew from this was that there was nothing but the passing scene of our experience – the mind 'in front' of it goes as firmly as the material thing 'behind' it, so to speak. This is a great simplification. We have only to reckon with the scene enacted on the stage without a producer out of sight or spectator in the pit – indeed, as Hume was himself not slow to point out, we do not really need the stage[1], there are just the scenes as they come, the world is a wholly one-tier world, there is no split-level here. Such scenes may indeed be thought to continue after the dissolution of our bodies, and we may be able to speak of some kind of identity in terms of relations between them, though this would appear to be harder in the absence of bodily impressions or their equivalent. But Hume himself, and most of his successors in the past, assumed that the passing show itself would end with the ending of sense impressions, and in that case, in his view, there would be nothing that could remain – there would be just nothing. And it was in the confident assurance that this was the fate which awaited him, inevitably in virtue of what we are and not because of any unkindly or hostile attitude of any other power towards us, that Hume drew to the close of his own life, with great self-possession and humour as we have seen.

The position adopted here by Hume is compatible with a distinction between extended and non-extended existence, and he himself based the distinction upon that between impressions of sight and touch, which alone give us the idea of extension, and those of sound, taste, smell and feeling which do not. There is here a frank admission of experiences or impressions which exist nowhere, and this is significant. But there is no recognition of any reality that is not reducible to our primary data of sensations, feelings and images; and, therefore, whatever else may be said about us there is no being or entity distinct from the course of our passing experience and which remains constant as the scene changes. On this score Hume was quite explicit, for the simple reason that he could find no such being. The words in which he put this are very familiar, but they go so much to the heart of the matter that we can well afford to quote them again:

For my part, when I enter most intimately into what I

call *myself*, I always stumble on some particular perception or other, of heat or cold, light or shade, love or
hatred, pain or pleasure. I can never catch *myself* at the
time without a perception, and never can observe any
thing but the perception. When my perceptions are
removed for any time, as by sound sleep, so long am I
insensible of *myself*, and may truly be said not to exist.[2]

It is hard not to sympathise with this so long as the
undertaking is conducted in the way Hume himself understood it. For, as I have stressed already, when we turn in to
look into ourselves we seem to find nothing, not even the
perceiving, in any way distinct from having the impression,
the colour and the smells and so forth just being there; and
in some recent positions very similar to those of Hume, like
some versions of 'neutral monism' and phenomenology, the
insistence on there being nothing but the passing scene,
nothing at all behind or in front, is very explicit.

And yet there appears to be an Achilles' heel in this kind
of philosophy, for even Hume is forced to admit that we
make sense of our environment in terms of certain
relations – of contiguity and so forth – which hold between
our sensations. How are these apprehended? If there is only
the passing scene there appears to be no way in which the
impressions which have occurred in the past could make
any impact on my present experience. I shall be the slave of
the moment. But since it is admitted that the patterns of my
experience create a strong expectation in me that events
will follow a certain course, I must somehow be able to
transcend the present, there must be more than the passing
scene; and the vital question is – just what is this more?

This was one of the main thoughts that occurred to Kant
when Hume, in Kant's famous words, had awakened him
from his 'dogmatic slumber'. The slumber meant going
along with what had been generally taken for granted about
the world and ourselves, especially in rationalist philosophy. But scepticism like that of Hume proved very disturbing until Kant settled upon one basic consideration in
the sea of doubt, namely that we are aware in our experience of some kind of world of objects. We make sense of

things, and life as we know it would not be possible if we did not. To be the slave of the passing scene would be like being in some kind of delirium, not, indeed, even that, but more like the first moment of coming round from a fainting fit when things have no shape or solidity at all, just a fog. We can in fact hardly conceive what totally unorganised experience would be like. But in that case two things seem to follow. The first is that things should not happen in a purely random way in the world as we know it, it must be subject to some laws or system which make it possible to correlate and identify things and manipulate them. We may not know how this comes about, and so far as the present point is concerned, there is no guarantee that it will continue. But life as we know it is only possible subject to these conditions, and we presuppose them as much in exact science as in every-day activity. But secondly, we must be aware of these unities and regularities. We must know before and after, by whatever name, and to the right and left; and whatever this and the like may imply further – about space and time and so forth, on which Kant made some very shrewd observations also – one thing seems certain, namely that there must be someone or something at the centre of such experience to hold the terms and relations of it together in one consciousness.

But what in turn, we must continue to ask, could this something be? It cannot itself be something like the world which is held together in consciousness – or any item of it. It cannot itself be known as they are known, for it is itself the condition of their being known. It is bound to be somehow behind the scenes and cannot be subject to the conditions by which things are known, namely that they should be limited or bounded and so identified in distinction from one another. We cannot tie down or place the organising centre of experience in that way and make it just one other object among the things we apprehend. It is not known as things are known but as a condition of knowing, and as Kant was very anxious not to fall foul again of Hume's sort of difficulties, he tended to end up with something which, while of the utmost importance and quite unavoidable, seemed to have no character or tangible reality at all, a principle as he in fact sometimes called it, an 'imaginary focus', a centre which had to function but which could hardly be more than a centre. Kant also held that because there was some incompleteness about the way we apprehend things, or because they were known within the conditions of our having our kind of experience, including modifications of our own senses, we could not know things as they were 'in themselves'; and this, understood in some ways, gets perilously near that bifurcation of being from which Berkeley seemed to have delivered us in his criticism of Locke's doctrine of material substances. There is, in fact, a tendency towards a radical bifurcation in the whole of Kant's philosophy. How far Kant meant it in that way is a moot point; it has been much debated and scholars will continue to do so. Some of the main difficulties in Kant's treatment of other subjects stem from this source. But we cannot pursue that theme here. Suffice it to note that for Kant there were, in some sense 'things in themselves' as well as things as we apprehend them, and the former, while their existence has to be recognised, remain entirely unknown to us. This affords some location also, in a metaphorical sense, for whatever it is (also in its way a 'something we know not what') by which the unity of our experience is sustained. But this does not warrant any inference from the recognition of a subject of experience to its nature; and to the extent that we can place it in the world of things in themselves,[3] that only accentuates the fact that, although it has to be postulated, it remains entirely unknown.[4]

Kant does also refer to an empirical or appearance self, but this is understood in terms of the inner arrangement of the data presented to us from without and fleeting emotions and desires, and has no permanent element. It is for this reason that the category of substance cannot, according to Kant, be applied to this appearance self.

A great deal of subsequent philosophy turned on the bifurcation in Kantian philosophy and the question of how, if at all, it might be healed. Some found hints of further progress in Kant himself, or in some particular way of understanding him. Kant himself was certainly averse to leaving the idea of things in themselves a total blank, and he contended that we could reduce the mystery in some respects by looking to the implications, not of knowledge but of what seemed equally unmistakable to him, namely that we have moral obligations. This did not give us knowledge proper or 'theoretical' knowledge, for the only knowledge of that kind we can have is the knowledge of things as they are in experience. But we can have 'practical' knowledge in the sense that we have reason to postulate certain things, on the basis of our moral experience, about the world as it extends 'beyond' our experience, and this would include the belief in our freedom as moral agents, in the reality of God and of our immortality also as a requirement of the fulfilment of an ideal we cannot fully realize at present. It is not to the purpose at the moment to do more than recognise these further claims, though the last of them will be noted again later. But for the moment we must not stray too far from the problem of the mysterious intractable character of whatever it is that is required by Kant to account for the unity or system of our experience.

Kant himself used certain terms in this context, and used them regularly, which are suggestive of some kind of thing or entity, for example 'self' and 'subject'. He qualified this by the word 'pure' and so we have the doctrine of the 'pure self' or the 'pure ego', and it is this 'pure ego' or 'noumenal self' which is active in moral experience. But it is a moot point how much this really adds to the notion of a 'unifying centre', a 'focus' or, in somewhat elaborate Kantian terminology, 'transcendental unity of apperception'. We have indeed made progress, for it is a considerable advance, a 'turning of the tables on Hume' as some have put it, to be assured that there really must be *something* at least which makes possible the unification of experience. But can we not go further? Is there no further hold we can get of the self as subject?

For a great many thinkers after Kant the answer was 'No'. They took their cue from Hegel who held that the bifurcation in Kantian philosophy need not be absolute; for the distinction between things as they seem and things as they are (appearance and reality) is, in fact, a distinction between things as they seem in a limited understanding of them and as they are when their nature is fully unfolded. The world 'beyond' is the completion of the limited world of present experience, and although we may not, in our present limitations, get a proper grasp of what this complete or 'ultimate' reality is like, we do have a clue in that very unification which is the constituent principle of our having a world of experience at all. Ultimate reality must be a whole and, as it is reason which seems to render possible the unification of present experience, the ultimate principle of all reality would seem to be reason – 'the real is the rational'. We arrive in this way at an idea of the whole universe as one complete whole in which everything finds its completion by rational necessity. Finite things, the world around us and ourselves, are appearances, modes or limitations of this One. The name for this type of philosophy is monism. There are other sorts of monism, and note will be taken of that later. But, in the type of post-Hegelian idealism which dominated philosophical thought in the later part of the nineteenth century, the self was apt to be taken as a limitation of a whole whose essence was rational coherence and would thus be regarded as itself a mode or centre of unification within the whole.

This gives us a somewhat rarefied view of the self. But that thought was not found very daunting by leading idealist thinkers. T. H. Green, sometimes known as 'the father of English idealism', found it possible to conceive of the universe as 'a system of all-inclusive relations' sustained in being by an 'eternal consciousness' or Spiritual Principle which also 'reproduces' itself in us in the form of 'a self-distinguishing consciousness', which holds together the facts of experience which exist as facts only in the relatedness thereby made possible. Other idealists sought to do more justice to the 'given' factor in experience and avoided the abstraction of mere relatedness. But the self tended to be taken all the same in its function of unification and as a mode of the unification of one comprehensive system. This raised many problems, especially concerning the presumed independence or initiative or responsibility of finite beings. For, if we are no more than partial exemplifications of the unity of the whole, everything seems to be prescribed by the rational necessity which holds the whole together; and, even if we go beyond this and conclude with Bradley that the ultimate necessitation is more than merely rational, the initial problem remains that all is determined by the whole to which we belong. Indeed, all evil tends to be dismissed, in this type of metaphysics, as unreal or illusory, as in some Oriental systems of thought and religion which, in this regard, have a close affinity with the prevailing absolutist metaphysics of the late nineteenth century.

In the light of these problems, many idealist writers, deeply concerned as the whole movement was with ethical problems and our accountability, laid particular stress on the function which finite persons have as distinct centres of unification within the whole. This, as in the case of thinkers like Pringle-Pattison and G. F. Stout and A. E. Taylor, brought the main position into closer accord with what we feel normally bound to think of ourselves; but that advantage seemed to be gained at the expense of consistency, and some very notable idealists, like Bernard Bosanquet, seemed to have the better of the argument in the fairly sharp domestic controversies which ensued. For if we remain no more than 'finite centres of unification' there remains little of the distinctness and power of initiative for which such eloquent pleas were made by other idealists; and if we are driven to think of our own function, in the unification of experience, on the famous analogy of a number of peep holes being gradually enlarged until all who look through them view exactly the same scene, we have, in this overlapping or confluence of selves, an eventual elimination of the finite person by his absorption into the whole. That was for many idealists the destiny in which we would realize ourselves in due course.

Refinements and ramifications of idealist or absolutist metaphysics cannot be considered closely here. But it will be evident that one major factor, in this way of thinking of human life and its significance, is the very formal or abstract conception of the self in terms of its function in making us aware of a unified world of objects. There seems to be nothing 'in between' to hold us apart; the boundaries of experience are fluid and overlap as different parts of a jig-saw puzzle may be put together. Distinctness is relative and partial or provisional. But this seems, all the same, sharply at odds with the way each of us normally thinks of himself. We do somehow think of ourselves as beings in our own right, however much we may acknowledge our indebtedness to others and to society. We could not, admittedly, exist without other people and the world we inhabit, we could not *be* in a void; and there seems to be more than a recognition of causal factors here. There may even be some sense in which our responsibilities are shared, though that is a very tricky question. But when every allowance of this sort has been made, there remains the very firm impression that everyone of us has some kind of being or actual reality to which the idea of 'a centre' or 'focus' or 'principle' seems hardly to do proper justice. It is not merely that each man's experience and history are different; it is not just the content of each one's experience that makes him different. He is a different man. Or so at least we are usually inclined to think.

The idea of 'a pure self' or 'pure Ego', a subject which is always subject and never object, was developed also in the late nineteenth century by a small number of eminent thinkers, influenced especially by Lotze, who did not subscribe to absolutist metaphysics, though they could hardly be quite uninfluenced by it, and who approached the subject in a very different way. Two outstanding names here are James Ward and F. R. Tennant, contemporaries at Cambridge for a long period. The starting point for both of them was science and a cautious empiricism. But in the course of a careful review of what the facts of our experience, including the long course of human evolution, are like, and leading to what Tennant described as 'interpretative belief', which is continuous with inductive science, both found it impossible to avoid recognising a subject of experience which is always a subject and cannot, for that reason it was thought, be directly known. 'Thinking implies a thinker', but the thinker, in that case, is inferred. 'The subject of experience, is, as knower, precluded from being immediately known.'[5] Nor could it be known at all in detachment from some reality which is known. Ward continues:

> The reality is experience. We allow that it is a unity but it is at once a unity that implies a duality and a duality that implies a unity. O to be known must surely be and S to know must surely also be. Again, O, as known, implies a knower; and S, as knowing, implies a known. Both these factors of experience then are real, but only one is 'known' *in so far as known connotes object.*[6]

This goes also, according to Ward, for the activities of the subject, of which there are two main divisions, attending and feeling. Ward maintains that we bring about changes in the external world by the way we attend to things, taking what is known as ideo-motor action as his paradigm example. Certain bodily movements come about by our attending to them. But the process (or 'acts') of attention is not itself introspectible. We know it only in the changes which it brings about; and likewise the feelings which largely determine the set of our attention are not directly known but are inferred from their effects upon our thought and behaviour. The subject can thus never 'be the direct object of its own experience'. It is known through the way it is involved in the kind of experience we have.

At the same time Ward is equally insistent that the self which we do come to know in this way has to be something. It is an actual individual self. 'Let the substantiality of this being be interpreted how it may, the actuality of it is past question.'[7] It is not 'a mere *focus imaginarius* – a psychological fiction like the physicist's fiction "centre of force" '. If it were we would have the contradiction of a relation with only one term. This point is so important for Ward, and it brings us so much to the crux of our problem, that I shall here venture to quote a somewhat lengthy passage in which the present points are very explicitly made. Ward wrote:

> It would come nearer to our crucial question if the objection just considered were amended by asking with what right we make an intellectual abstraction the subject of an existential proposition. There is certainly no such

right, and the psychologists who substitute the abstract 'consciousness' for the concrete conscious subject, alone forget this. The I of the 'I am', the sole text of the 'rational psychology' that Kant criticized and equally the I of the 'I think' of Descartes' *cogito ergo sum*, if taken as a *res completa*, is an abstraction. But that pure subject or Ego which we reach in our analysis of experience at its rational level stands for no abstraction so long as we are content to distinguish it without attempting to separate it from its objective complement, the non-Ego. When in some supreme issue a man affirms himself saying, like Caesar crossing the Rubicon or Luther entering Worms, 'I will', to tell him then that this I of which he speaks is *itself* an utter abstraction, because our *concept* of it is the limit of a long process of intellection – surely this would be outrageous.[8]

In his more metaphysical writings, and especially *The Realm of Ends*, Ward presents a general picture of the universe which is not unlike the monadology of Leibniz except that for Ward individual monads did really interact. This was his answer to the Absolutist monism of his day. But we shall not follow his work further here into this more speculative field. Suffice it to note the insistence on a genuine or actual self of which, however, we know nothing besides the requirement of it in our analysis of experience.

For here, although we seem to be getting very close to our quarry, there still appears to be something lacking. Some important contemporary thinkers would find the way forward by taking Ward's own insistence that we know attention and feeling only in the effect they have on our behaviour in a more wholehearted way than Ward and so settle the problem by just dissolving the self into the appropriate behaviour, and we shall be noting their view in a moment. But if we find ourselves unable to take that course, there remains the feeling that, even to refer to the self as an implicate or condition of experience, the self must somehow be accessible to us in some other way. Can we refer to any process or entity at all without some means of determining what it is in itself? Can we have a meaningful concept of something which is only known obliquely?

It might be thought that the answer here could be 'Yes', in as much as we do postulate many things in science of which we know nothing beyond their being required to explain something else. But this would be misleading. For any forces or entities postulated in this way are never wholly mysterious to us. They have to be thought of in one sort of way for the explanation to have point. This is very plain when we postulate a hitherto invisible star to account for the established movements of other stars – we know what it is to be a star. But, even if we think of much more intangible entities, we have to characterise them up to some point in terms of what we do know to fit them, as explanatory factors, into the total pattern of what we are seeking to understand. There is surely nothing to be done with entities of which no characterisation at all is possible.

There could perhaps be one exception to this, namely the idea of God. For here, it is commonly thought, we have the idea of a Being who is altogether 'beyond' or 'outside' the world as we can understand it, a transcendent Being. God is thus thought to account for the world, not in the sense in which one thing normally helps to explain the occurrence of another by being related to it in a system, but in the sense of being accountable, in a way of which therefore we can form no precise idea, for there being such a system. God, on this view, is thus totally mysterious in his essential nature, though we are able, indeed required, to think that he must *be*. How in spite of this, it is possible, in some oblique way, to make further more precise affirmations about God does not concern us now – it is a large problem in itself. For what I most want to add now is that, although there may well be illuminating analogies between our knowledge of ourselves or of one another and our knowledge of God, we are not total mysteries to ourselves or to one another. Even if we speak metaphorically, in some context, of transcending ourselves, this is a very different use of the term from the way God is thought to transcend the finite world. The case of God is unique, and while, in this very special case, it may be proper to refer to a being of whose nature we are not able to say anything expressly, this does not hold in the same way or for similar reasons of anything else.

But how then can we break the deadlock? The self is actual, it is maintained, but it cannot be located or identified in the way some other entity in the world around us has to be characterised in some measure for us to be able to recognise it at all and know what is being talked about. Likewise, if the various experiences of the self can only be described in terms of their content, what are we to understand of the alleged experiencing itself? The answer is that the self, far from being a mysterious reality behind the scenes, is in fact what we know best. But we know it in a very special way in the very fact of being it and having the experiences we do have, including the activities we ourselves initiate. We do not, initially, know other persons in this way. We have to place them through our observation of their bodies or of some effect which begins with their bodies. But what we ascribe to them also, as must be stressed later, is the same sort of reality known to themselves as each one finds in his own case. We know ourselves and the course of our experiences in a way to which there is no proper parallel, uniquely. We know quite well what it is to have experience and to be ourselves, but we do not know it in the same way as we know anything else.

This does not mean that everything about a particular person is altogether clear to him. At a certain level there is a lot that we do not know about ourselves, and we shall note that also in a moment. But the way a person knows himself and his experiences initially is not mysterious in itself except in the sense that there is no further way in which it may be characterised. We do not know ourselves at this point by observation, or by anything resembling observation. There is nothing we detect in a way we can then point out or locate or describe; and the difficulty is that we are so accustomed, we might almost say conditioned, to learn about things by looking for them that we will persist, in the manner of Hume and in a way Locke before him, in 'turning into' ourselves to *look* for the self or observe and identify it and then of course find nothing. Nor do we have to conceive the enterprise in a strictly empiricist way in terms of Hume's impressions and ideas. It is the very notion of *looking* that is wrong, not because the self is a bare form and not actual, but because it is not known by turning in to peer at it in any sense at all.

One source of confusion here is that, once we are set on some search for the self, or for experience as a non-observable process, we tend to look for something which presents itself in some distinctive way on this or that occasion. But we do not find evidence for the self, or for the non-observable nature of experience, in any particular manifestation of either. They are the same in *all* experience. The content varies, but it is not on the basis of such variation that we settle what is involved in having *any* experience. If we were to speak in terms of evidence, the complication is, not the lack or paucity of it, but its abundance; it is everywhere, at least as far as experience goes. This is why the challenge made by Professor J. J. C. Smart, namely that we should provide examples of experiences which possess irreducibly 'psychic' properties, seems to miss the point. For it is not a case of some experiences being more obviously 'psychic' than others. They are all so – essentially.

In like manner, the use that is made, in this context, of the idea of introspection, is apt to be misleading. There is certainly such a thing as introspection. But what this means is that we can take note of the way we feel or think at various times, how we react to provocation, what makes us angry or pleased, and so forth. We discover in this way the same sort of thing, in essentials, as an outside observer might learn about us and of which, in some cases, the outside observer may be the better judge. But noting what we are like and do at various times is a very different matter from specifically looking in on ourselves, in the course of anything we do or undergo.

This is partly what is in the mind of those who maintain that what we need to invoke is not introspection but retrospection, that is taking note of an experience immediately it is over. But there are two different issues here. One is that if we pause in the course of some activity, or of something we undergo, like a feeling of anger or fear, this affects the course of that activity itself and we do not therefore have a fair expression of it. The observation at once complicates the situation. How far this applies, and how it operates in the practice of psychological study, does not concern us closely now. For there is the different issue, sometimes put in the form that the self as subject can never observe itself as an object for it is always essentially subject. The difficulties of introspection, in the first case, and the prospect of coping through retrospection, have little to do directly with the second. Nor does the idea of retrospection alleviate in any way the difficulty of those who feel that, when they 'turn into' themselves, they discover nothing. For it is not a case of the process of 'looking in' distracting attention or otherwise changing what goes on, it is simply that nothing can be found by looking in the way intended.

This is also why the celebrated notion of knowledge 'by acquaintance' does not quite suit the case here, though some have thought otherwise. For here again we have a suggestion of some kind of confrontation with something over against us. We come back, therefore, to the view to which Berkeley seemed to be pointing in his doctrine of notions as a special way in which we know ourselves, namely that the way we know the process of having experience and its being distinctively our experience, is in the very process itself and in being oneself having it. Knowledge of oneself is indissoluble from being oneself and known in a peculiar way in all experience. There are indeed occasions when we speak of being very self-conscious or, sometimes, self-aware. But this is again a different matter of being peculiarly aware of what our present states are like and of other people's attention or notice of us. But we are aware of ourselves, in the radical sense which is involved in our being ourselves, not just in special states of self-consciousness but even when we are least conscious of ourselves in the special sense in question, indeed equally and invariably in *all* experience, and for that reason quite unobtrusively. It is the constancy of our awareness of ourselves that has made some persons, conditioned or predisposed in reflective thought to look for something manifested in some more distinctive way, to seem to miss out on that awareness altogether.

This is the answer to those who might instance cases of complete absorption in what we are doing, or in some end to be attained, as in the case of running after the bus. Of what, it may be said, are we thinking in such cases other than of what we are doing and what pertains directly to that? But it is not in fact a case of thinking of oneself, and of the having of our experience, in the sense in which we might turn our attention to this or that, but of being aware, unreflectively and essentially, in the situations instanced, as in all others, of ourselves as the beings we are, having our present experience.

The reference to present experience brings us to a further formidable problem. For even if it is allowed that I am aware of my present experience as my own in the process of having it, the question still remains of how the experience of half an hour ago can be said to belong to me in the same way. How do we establish our continued identity? Before taking this question up further there are, however, a number of other objections to the position already presented, and these, although reflecting the misgivings of earlier thinkers, have been canvassed today in new and challenging terms. It will be well to look at these objections before we proceed, especially as I think it can be shown that they stem largely from the persistent supposition that our alleged awareness of ourselves is akin to the way we look at or observe other things.

4 Some Recent Views

One common objection to the position I have outlined hitherto is this. It is supposed that if we are in some way directly aware of ourselves and of our experience in having it, then we can never be mistaken or deluded about ourselves. This is a point that has been very vigorously put by the most celebrated critic of Cartesian dualism in our own time, namely Professor Gilbert Ryle, in *The Concept of Mind*. He draws attention to the fact that there are many things which our friends, or sometimes an expert like a psychiatrist, may discover about us which we do not know ourselves. We may think that we are very modest or easily frightened, but others who know us closely may judge otherwise. No one, I imagine, would wish to deny this and it is usually sound advice to try 'to see ourselves as others see us'. But, it is then argued, on the theory of some alleged 'private access' to ourselves, we ought not to be at any time under any misapprehensions about ourselves.

The sting can, however, be taken out of much of this argument from the start. For the kind of thing which our friends or others can point out to us about ourselves concern very largely, not what happens to go on at some particular time but what we are generally inclined to do or be. We all have traits of character or dispositions, and we characterise people on this basis as timid, benevolent, vicious and so forth. A disposition is like the general properties of external things; it is manifested, not all the time but in what happens to various things on certain occasions and what we learn generally about objects of that kind. The brittleness of the glass means that it will be easily shattered if struck, but it is not being shattered at the moment, and may never be. Likewise, I may not be angry now or timid, as there is no occasion to be either, but I may be a bad-tempered person or easily frightened. This we learn by noting how we ourselves or other persons react or conduct ourselves at various times. There is no reason in principle why everything we learn about ourselves in this way could not be discovered about us by other people, although in practice that is clearly ruled out. We do not learn about character and dispositions by inspecting them, as we might examine a machine to discover what it will do. I learn that someone is mean by noting how reluctant he is to give away money. But a dualist, defending in essentials the position of Descartes, can readily allow this. For all he has to claim is that there is some immediate awareness of our own mental states at the time they occur; in other respects he can admit to faulty judgment and delusion.

This applies to all that may be said about unconscious dispositions, set up perhaps by some forgotten event which has left us inclined to react in certain ways of which we have failed to take note ourselves. No one, therefore, who claims some immediate awareness of our own states at the time need hesitate to accept whatever of the teaching of Freud, for example, he finds established by the evidence. Whether there are unconscious actual states of mind is a further question, and it would take us far afield to consider what would in fact be involved in that possibility. But, if there should be such states, they present no problem for us at this point which does not appear alike over conscious states.

But what then of conscious states? Could we be wrong at the time in supposing that these occur to us? Yes, indeed, in some ways. We might be mistaken in some ways about the nature of the experience we are having. I might, for example, believe that I am hearing a footfall outside my door, only to discover later that it was only the boards creaking as the house cooled down at night. I may also give a bad or misleading description of what in fact I heard. But about the way it seems to me at the time I can hardly be in error, and I can hardly fail to be aware of having the experience I do have, even if it should be, in fact, very unobtrusive and little heeded in the main course of my attention and activities.

A question might be raised here about the familiar example of the ticking of the clock which we do not notice till it stops. But various explanations of this situation are possible. One might account for it entirely in physiological terms – the drums of our ears continue to be affected (and our nerves and brains) without making any actual difference to our consciousness at the time, but the change in the physical stimulus does stir up a change in consciousness. Alternatively we might say that we do actually hear the ticking but only faintly and without heeding it. In the same way we may have emotions, of fear or anger for example, of which we are certainly aware but of whose nature we do not take sufficient note at the time. So that it would be quite sensible, in terms of the claims I make in this context, for someone to point out to me that I was more frightened or angry than I realized at a particular time.

A further major objection, and one to which great prominence is given by Professor Ryle, concerns the relation of our alleged non-observable states and processes to the activities of our bodies, and the way we thereby make our purposes effective in the world. The view of Descartes, it will be recalled, was that the mind as a non-extended entity acted upon the body while the body in turn affected the mind. This seems to be a fact of common experience. What happens to me now, and the things I do, are largely determined by the state of my body. Sitting as I am, with my eyes open, I am bound to see certain things; and, maintaining my intention to go on with my work, I remain at my desk and my fingers move the pen across the page. But, it will be asked, if this means that my mental states influence my body and *vice versa*, how precisely does this come about? How does the one influence the other, by what media is the influence transmitted? Ryle puts this very forcibly when he writes: 'The actual transactions between the episodes of the private history and those of the public history remain mysterious, since by definition they can belong to neither series'[1]. If, then, we can form no conception of what the alleged 'transactions' could be like, how can we even affirm that they happen?

If the advocate of dualism takes this objection at its face

value, he is almost certain to give himself away. He will look for something to say about the mysterious 'transactions'; he will posit, perhaps, some ethereal substance or mind stuff or other medium to meet the case. But challenged to say what this could be like, or what evidence there is for it, he will be nonplussed; he can find no such evidence; and even if he could and it became established that there was some subtle medium of the sort required, this would only push the problem a stage further back, for we would have to explain how the 'transactions' make their impact on one side or the other, and so *ad infinitum* – as Ryle himself is not slow to point out. But surely the answer for the dualist is to say that he does not speak in terms of these transactions and has no need to postulate them. All he needs to say is that in point of fact we find that mental states do influence our bodies and that bodily states are found as a matter of experience to influence the mind. But are we not, then, left with a mystery, affirming something we cannot explain? Certainly, but this is not peculiar to the present case. In the last resort we are always bound to accept what we find to be the case. This is true of all causation. Hume pointed out the fallacy of looking for some link between cause and effect, and those, like Professor Ryle, who are not without much affinity with Hume, might have heeded him to better purpose here. We do not, admittedly, establish causal relations in isolation, but in terms of a very elaborate system which the scientist investigates in great detail, and we can in this way explain particular causal relations in considerable detail. But the fact remains that all this is what we find to be the way things happen or infer on the basis of what is already established in this way. We can offer no reason for the way things do occur in the world around us other than that this is in fact what we find.

We may of course have good reason to believe that the consistency and regularity of events is a necessary one, and not just something which happens. This is the famous problem of induction. Hume maintained that there was no intrinsic necessity in the way things occur, only a psychological one, an expectation created in us by the fortunate regularity in the way things have happened hitherto. To

answer Hume here without going outside the order of
nature itself is extremely difficult, and for my part, in spite
of celebrated efforts by various thinkers, I do not think we
establish any ultimate necessity without invoking the idea
of God. But however this may be, the discovery of particular causal relations is not affected. We still discover these
in the last resort by noting just what they are, presupposing
what experience hitherto confirms, uniformity and concomitant variation.

This is plainly so in the external world. But here, it will
be said, we are dealing with things of substantially the same
nature, namely physical things. Mind, on the present hypothesis, is radically different. How can things so radically
different affect one another? But why not? It is indeed
strange that, normally at least, it is only our own bodies
that we are able to influence directly. But this is what in
fact we find, and surely we cannot go back on what seems to
be an unmistakable and common feature of our experience
simply because we can say nothing further about it. We
cannot gainsay the facts, however perplexing; and in the
last resort they are no more perplexing than anything else
which the world presents. There is no ultimate explanation
of anything – short of God; and we must accept the world
as we find it.

The temptation to look for some way of accounting for
the relation between mind and body is understandable, and
there is some reason to suspect that Descartes himself
fell into it. He spoke of 'animal spirits' which arise within
the body and, at the pineal gland, transmit the influence
from the brain. These spirits, as some would understand
Descartes here, are of an ambiguous nature and not certainly mind or body, and might thus be thought to mediate
between the two. But they are of course inventions for which
we have no evidence, and it is by no means clear that Descartes himself intended the idea as a means of accounting
for the relation of mind and body. It could be no more than
an attempt to fill out what he knew about the body, and
likewise for his views about the pineal gland. Knowledge of
the body was still, by our standards, very elementary, and
Descartes might be at fault only in making what we now

know to be rather rash physiological speculations. I am strongly inclined to think this.

It should be added here, to avoid misunderstanding, that we can indeed, in one sense, explain a good deal of the way the mind influences the body, and the reverse. We can fill out the story very fully on the physiological side and are learning more and more about it. We can describe the nervous system and the way the muscles grip the bones, etc., and the expert can tell us a great deal today about the way the brain functions. But all this is still to tell more and more of the story on its physiological side. We can likewise discover more about the way our thoughts shape themselves and fill out our knowledge of logic or psychology in other ways. But this does nothing, on either side, to explain why, when the brain is in a certain state, we have certain experiences, nor why, when the mind is disposed in some way, certain changes in the brain, and thereby in the rest of the body, come about. There may of course be resemblances between the operations of the brain and certain mental activities, although this would to my mind be very hard to establish. But there would still be nothing here which would reduce the radical difference between thought or experience, on the one hand, and physical states of the brain on the other—or thereby the mystery of the way the one affects the other as we find to be the case.

The objection with which we are dealing now has been put a little differently by Professor John Passmore. He observes that 'the only force the mind has at its disposal is spiritual force, the power of rational persuasion; and the only thing that can move it is a purpose'. On the other hand, bodies can 'only push'. A body does not 'push' the mind. But surely we are talking again of what goes on on one side or the other of the dichotomy. No one claims that the mind gives the body a 'push' or that any other physical explanation of the mind's influence is possible. All that is held is that the influence is somehow real. Likewise, when Professor Hirst asks: 'How can the spatial characteristics of physical things be reproduced in the unextended non-spatial mind?'[2] this is again a misrepresentation. Physical things do not have to become mental, or somehow enter the mind, *qua* physical things, to condition or influence the mind. They remain what they are but are found, as a fact of experience, to have the influence we note. The objection we have been considering, in its formulation by Hirst and Passmore, highlights the tendency to consider what is said about states of mind in terms which are appropriate only to physical things, as in the case of those who 'turn into' the mind to 'look' at it.

We shall have to return again to the question of the precise way the mind is involved with its body. But in the meantime let us note a further major objection, in many respects the most crucial one, to our main position. This is the objection that, if the mind is taken to be radically different in nature from external or physical reality, then there is no way in which it can be in contact with any reality other than itself. Descartes may in some respects have laid himself open to this objection. This is because of the somewhat rarefied view which, as we saw earlier, he took of the self as a thinking thing, combined with the ambiguous status of sensible perceptions as he conceived them. Colours, sounds, smells, etc. did not, as we noted, belong to the sphere of the intellect for Descartes, but neither were they strictly physical—the essence of matter is extension. The mind tends thus to be wrapped up in itself, and Descartes could only get out of this 'ego-centric predicament', as it is described, by seeking first to prove the existence of God by severely rationalist arguments and then invoking the veracity of God to guarantee our strong inclination to think that perception puts us in touch with the physical world. This is a somewhat strained procedure and not too easily reconciled with Descartes' initial programme to proceed only by clear and distinct ideas of reason—perception being for him in the area of 'confused ideas'.

Other thinkers, however, as we have also seen, in insisting upon some kind of pure ego have been quite emphatic that the self is effectively in contact with some reality other than itself. Tennant puts it very strongly: 'Knowledge of the self and knowledge of the world are interdependent from the first stages which we can trace, and grow *pari passu*'[3]. Most would agree that, in sense experience, we are in touch with external reality. How this comes about will vary from one view to another. Some would maintain with Berkeley that the world we know in perception is the world of our own presentations as these become necessary for us and are co-ordinated. For others these presentations lead us, directly or indirectly, to a quite independent material world. We need not enter the debate, and we would have to stray far afield if we did so, important though the topic is in itself. For the main point is that we take ourselves to be, in perception, in touch with the world around us, and thereby also with other persons. This may not be the only way in which we are in touch with other persons. For the claim is made by some that we have telepathic communications with one another. It may of course be that telepathy can only operate where persons are already known and identified otherwise (cf. below, p. 125). But in any case we normally know other persons by what we observe of them through their bodies. The way this comes about will have to be considered more closely later, as it obviously has considerable bearing on the possibility of existence independently of our present bodies, or perhaps in some totally disembodied way (see below, Chapter 9). But all we need note at the moment is that, in insisting that mental reality is altogether different from material reality, and that we know our own mental states in having them, we are in no way precluded from regarding ourselves as effectively in touch with the world and other persons.

This must be our reply to the points made very forcibly by Professor Ryle when he contends that the affirmation of what he calls, not very happily I have maintained, 'private access' commits us to solipsism, the view that we have no grounds for believing that anyone exists besides oneself. As Ryle rather dramatically puts it, on the Cartesian view 'absolute solitude is the ineluctable destiny of the soul'[4]. If this objection held the dualist position would clearly collapse. No one seriously believes that he is the only person in the world. Life would be impossible without other people, and it has been held that a serious solipsist would go out of his mind, which does not seem improbable unless he is of the confused kind, like the lady who wrote to Bertrand Russell to say that she had been convinced of the soundness of solipsism and was surprised that there were not more people who agreed! There are, indeed, well-known difficulties of accounting for our knowledge of one another, as the words 'the problem of other minds' indicates. But any position which clearly ruled out the possibility of a solution would stand condemned. But the dualist position has no such consequence.

If, of course, the claim to 'private access' or its like meant that we could only know mental reality by such access, then Ryle's objection would be irrefutable. We do not have 'private access' to other minds. Even in telepathy, if it exists, we would not know other minds in the same way as we know our own. But there is no reason to suppose that mental reality can only be known in one sort of way. The person who claims that he knows his own thoughts in having them is in no way precluded from maintaining that we have some different mediated knowledge of other minds – or other kinds of knowledge of one's own mind. The form of the mediation, or whatever else may be said in this context, is another matter; and we shall return to this problem. But in the meantime it can be noted that there is nothing in the dualist position as such which cuts us off from the world and other persons. A dualist is not bound to be a solipsist.

Two further features of Professor Ryle's attack on dualism of mind and body can be most conveniently noted here. He seems to take the view that the alleged mental states to which the dualist refers must be detached atomic episodes, erupting from time to time in the course of our observable behaviour. He thus asks very wittily: 'How many acts of will did you perform before breakfast?' 'At what moment was the boy going through the volition to take the high dive?' A naive reader is apt to be very nonplussed by these questions. I did many things before breakfast, shaved, dressed, read my letters, etc. I could not add to this that I also performed acts of will, as if these were activities to be conceived in the same way and existing side by side with shaving, etc. The proper answer is that I was maintaining my intention to do all the things I did as I was doing them. Purposing is not something over and above shaving or dressing and in competition with them. The shaving is a purposive activity itself, but it does not consist in merely bodily movements. I continue to will these movements, and I could stop them at any time. There is no conscious effort to do this, although I might have 'to bring myself', as we say, to do it. Normally, once embarked on a fairly obvious task, I just get on with it. At other times I may have a very hard struggle to do something or bring myself to start it, and we speak of making an effort or taking a decision in these and similar situations. But it is not on special occasions of this kind alone that we are purposing; our actions are purposive always, and I could not do anything without maintaining my intention to do it. Even when we do things absent-mindedly as we say 'without thinking much', as when I walk to the station with my mind on some work I have to do, the strictly physical behaviour is directed by my continuous purpose although I give little of my thought to it. Otherwise it would be a reflex action or some quite inexplicable movement of my limbs. To revert to the examples cited above, there is no particular point at which the boy performs the volition to dive. He just dives, but this means that he continues to purpose all his bodily movements all the time when he is making them.

Likewise with the course of our thoughts. These are not normally discrete and disjointed; they just flow, and at any particular time there is a great deal that goes on in my mental life. For the past half hour my thoughts have been mainly on what I am writing, but they have strayed from time to time and returned again to the main theme. I have also been aware of my surroundings, sometimes more vividly, sometimes less so; my attention is sometimes caught by the scene out of the window, and at other times I hardly look at it. I have been mildly aware of bodily sensations as my body presses on the chair and my elbow on the table and so on, and there are internal somatic sensations in my body. My mental life has been a varied multiform one in which my attention has sometimes been more, sometimes less, concentrated, flowing, expanding, and contracting like a stream with many currents and whirls and eddies. Nor is there any moment at which I am just thinking or being in some other way cognitively active. There is an emotional toning to my thoughts and activities and the continuous sustaining of my intention to keep my attention as it is or to change it and do whatever else is involved in all I have been doing all the time. A proper distinction may indeed be drawn between, for example, thinking and willing, but neither happens, without the other. Nor is there any sharp alternation of the two. It is thus a travesty of what the serious defender of dualism maintains today when it is supposed that he reduces the mental life, which he contrasts with physical changes, to discrete states of thinking or willing. He holds, on the contrary, that there is a real mental *life* which is continuously affecting our bodily state and being affected by it.

On its positive side, Professor Ryle's theme is that our activities, of whatever sort, can be entirely comprehended in terms of our visible behaviour and the dispositions which govern it. We have seen what is meant by a disposition, and it is certain that our lives would be unintelligible in the absence of fairly sustained dispositions, our likes and dislikes and other proclivities we have. These change, but if they had no relative permanence, if they changed in a quite random fashion, there would be no sense or consistency in what we did. Professor Ryle is not the first to stress this. Indeed, it is given special prominence by Aristotle. But Ryle has done important service in bringing the idea of dispositions to the centre in the philosophy of mind. His mistake, as it seems to me, is to suppose that, when he has reckoned with observable behaviour and dispositions, he has told the whole story. He has in fact left out the main item, namely the actualising of our dispositions in various ongoing mental processes. When I sweeten my tea with sugar you can explain this in terms of my fondness for sweet things or in particular for sugar or tea sweetened with sugar. This is not a causal explanation, it is not conceived in terms of antecedent events. But my action can also be accounted for in terms of mental occurrences. I see the cup of tea, this is a perceptual experience in which there is a great deal of understanding of what tea is like, etc. But there is also my experienced anticipation of what it will be like to drink my tea and my felt desire at the time that this should come about. The felt desire is not the state of my body as the thought of tea affects my gastric juices or the watering of my mouth, nor is it any marked emotional state, since I do not normally get highly excited by the thought of a cup of tea. But there is the experienced wanting which passes easily, in the absence of any inhibiting thought, into the intention to sweeten my tea and drink it. All this is normally very unobtrusive. But I would not sweeten my tea if that did not appeal to me, and 'appeal' refers here not merely to my fondness for sweetened tea which we establish from experience as a generalisation about me, but also to the immediate actualisation of this disposition in an actual modification of my state of mind at the time. In the absence of this it is hard to see what the disposition itself could be other than some state of my body. Ryle would not, I think, say that it is a state of my body. We have a generalisation based on observed behaviour. But it would be odd, to say the least, to suppose that the disposition could make itself felt in any other way than by actualising itself in the first instance in some mental state.

It may seem artificial to analyse our conduct in terms of thoughts and wants and of dispositions that govern these. In any normal situation things continue for us as if there were one unbroken process, and we do not for this reason usually refer to more than the one activity as a whole. That is why the appeal to ordinary language, of which more in a moment, is plausible and also misleading. It could be a perfectly adequate account of what I have just been doing to say that I have been working, or that I have been writing at the table. But a moment's reflection also assures us that working or writing involves more at the time than the movements of my fingers and other bodily changes, and this more is not solely what may be said about my interests and habits of thought, it is mainly the occurrent mental life through which I have been passing, my actual flow of thoughts, feelings, etc. together with the close integration of these with the bodily effects I intend and the causal conditions of my mental processes in states of my body as well as in their own proper development. To leave out the ongoing mental state, and speak only of dispositions, is to give us 'Hamlet' without the Prince.

I have attempted a close critical discussion of Professor Ryle's thesis elsewhere, and I shall not dwell further upon it here. Suffice it to note that while Ryle is not an outright materialist, in the sense of straightway telling the whole story of our conduct in terms of nerves, muscles, states of the brain and so on, he leaves us nothing besides the observable physical behaviour and certain more or less consistent dispositions. The purposing, which makes our conduct other than mechanical or accidental, is thought of entirely in terms of dispositions, and however ingeniously (and Ryle is a very ingenious thinker indeed) this is extended to cover the cases where, as in the case of Rodin's *Penseur*, we seem rapt in thought, it just goes against the obvious facts of everyone's experience, namely that we have mental processes of which each person is aware at the time in the very fact of having them. Consciousness authenticates itself in immediate experience.

There are however critics of dualism who take a much less extreme line than Ryle. They avoid the reductionism of his main thesis while also maintaining that no proper wedge can be driven between mind and body. A notable recent example is Professor P. F. Strawson, although it is not very clear that he deviates as sharply from Ryle in the last analysis as might at first appear. He admits, indeed he insists, that properly mental predicates as well as physical predicates may be affirmed about us. Thus, it could be said of me now that I am five feet eight inches tall and that I am thinking about philosophy. But both these predicates, Strawson contends, are affirmed about the same subject. The subject in both cases is 'I'. This, however, hardly takes us beyond ordinary language again. We do indeed say 'I am tall' as well as 'I am thinking', but this is just the most convenient locution for normal purposes. The distinctions which pervade our whole experience do not have to be reflected in what we say for day to day purposes. Likewise, when I say 'I opened the door' the dual character of the event does not have to be reflected in the terms I use. It would be foolishly cumbersome to say that I formed the intention to move to the door, etc. and my body in fact responded. The simpler terms suffice, but they do so without prejudice to the account we would give of the situation in philosophical reflection.

A more sophisticated argument adduced by Strawson refers to the involvement of people's bodies in any knowledge we have of them. We know other people through their bodies. It seems therefore that the body is essentially involved in our knowledge of persons, and for this reason an absolute wedge cannot be drawn between mental and physical reality. The ultimate unit is the person of whom mental and physical predicates are affirmed. It is difficult to grasp the full implications of this argument. But it seems to have one fatal weakness, namely the very dogmatic assumption that one sort of thing can only be known in one sort of way. The dualist will affirm that he knows his own mind in a very different way from that in which he knows other minds, and that this is fundamental in our knowledge of mental reality. Even if Strawson's argument held, the most that it would prove is that bodies are, in fact, indispensable to us. It could still be maintained that the essential component is the mind.

In line with his main approach to the subject, Strawson also notes that, when we observe people engaged in some activity, we do firmly say that we observe this activity. We see a man coiling a rope. But again this is the short convenient utterance we need for day to day purposes. What matters for our normal concern is that the man is coiling a rope, not hoisting a sail. But we do not strictly see the activity which makes the action a properly purposive one; the intention is presumed from the movement of the hands. Without the presumed intention and all that goes on which we do not strictly see there would be no action in the proper sense at all. The appeal to language, and even more generally to what is described as 'the structure of language', cannot settle our problem in disregard of the way mental processes are known to have the sort of reality they do have in our own experience in having them.

Strawson's position lies, somewhat uncertainly it seems to me, between the behaviourism of Ryle and the position which is usually known today as 'the identity thesis'. On most versions of the latter view, there is a frank admission of mental processes as something to which everyone has, in his own case, some immediate or private 'access', to keep to the usual but, as I have noted, somewhat misleading term. My being in pain is not exhaustively described by pain-behaviour such as screaming or rushing for some remedy. There is something which I just feel or experience, and the same is true of intellectual operations, though the admission is a little more grudgingly made in those cases. But it is also maintained that what I apprehend in this immediate fashion is, in fact, the same as the body which is open to the public observation of all. For the former there has now been coined the somewhat inelegant term 'raw feels'. There are then raw feels, but on examination we find that these are also in their turn bodily.

One version of this general position is called 'the double aspect' thesis. Mind and body, on this view, are two aspects of the same reality, a position which owes something to Spinoza's idea of one reality expressed in a number of attributes, an infinite number on his account. On one common version of the double aspect thesis the thoughts and feelings which I apprehend inwardly or privately are also in fact processes in the brain which the neurologist can observe in scientific study or 'from without'. This appears to concede what common sense requires in the way of recognising our own awareness of our mental life, and its efficacy, while holding on to the view that there is no properly non-material reality or any reality which is not open to public inspection.

One prominent feature in the commendation of this view is the contention that experience itself is neutral regarding the status of what goes on in our mental life. As Professor R. J. Hirst puts it: 'We have only evidence of certain experiences and activities, of ourselves thinking and seeing. There is no revelation of the ontological status of these activities or of the self which performs them.' It is only in subsequent reflection, in philosophical theorising mainly, that the question whether the activities are physical or mental properly arises. In some versions of this argument reference is made to Berkeleyan arguments about the status of the external world. Ordinary thought does not raise the question of the sense in which the 'furniture' of the world around us is real, it just takes it that things are 'there'. When we begin to think about perspectival distortions, about the pillar-box looking small in the distance or the round tower square, it is then that we begin to ask any questions, and some never get round to asking these questions at all. But this is in fact not a very good example to take, for it concerns what is on all accounts in some way external, it is in short a percept and not the perceiving that is involved; and whether or not Berkeley was right in supposing that nothing external exists except as perceived is irrelevant to the status of what is at issue properly in our present argument, namely whether the perceiving itself is an essentially non-material process. It seems to many, myself among them, that mental processes are known, in having them, to be radically different in nature from any external extended reality. The question of identity in this sense just does not arise; my thoughts at the moment are not the kind of thing which the physiologist as such can observe. However skilfully he may examine my brain he does not *see* my thoughts, emotions, etc. He may see some pointer to them, and, if he could make his science far more complete than it is at present, he might even read off some mental states from states of the brain; but he does not directly observe mental states, for they are not the kind of thing which can be observed.

This must be our answer also to Professor J. J. C. Smart when he claims that experiences are 'topic-neutral'. He admits that there is 'pure inner experience' to which 'only I have direct access'. But the status of such experience remains open. We do not, indeed, mean by 'experience' a brain process, but when we understand better we learn that what we initially described neutrally as 'what is going on in me' is in fact a process in the brain. The main weight of the argument is on the known correlation of brain processes and states of mind, but even if it could be shown that this correlation is complete (and we are very far from doing so, as Smart admits) that would still not make a thought or any other experience itself physical, whatever else might follow.

Smart invokes the analogy of lightning which we see as a flash of light but know to be 'an electric charge'. But even at its own level this is misleading, for it is only in a special sense, involving certain causal conditions, that the flash is also an electric charge. The use of such analogies does nothing to reduce what we expressly know to be the radically different nature of 'what goes on' as experience to any state of physical matter like the brain. If others think otherwise we can do nothing but agree to differ, to our great perplexity when what seems so plain to one is not so to others. The demand to break the deadlock by challenging the dualist to produce some unmistakably psychic experience is found by the dualist, as was noted earlier, to miss the point, since he finds *all* experience essentially psychic.

Those who defend some form of the identity thesis today owe a great deal to Professor Herbert Feigl. He is quite emphatic that we must recognise 'the privacy of immediate experience' and that to deny this, or deny the causal efficacy of mental states, is 'to fly in the face of the commonest of evidence'. He reminds the reductionist that he, like everyone else, will want anaesthesia for an operation. But he also holds that the 'raw feels' of immediate experience belong to 'a referent'. The account of the referent is not easy to follow. Sometimes it reminds us of Locke's unobserved material substance, but it is also in some way continuous with the 'raw feels'. Physical states have their referent also. But, in the case of our mental states and that of states of our bodies, the referent could well be the same. That it is, in fact, the same is established by a very arbitrary use of Occam's razor, namely that we must not invoke more entities than are strictly necessary, also called the principle of parsimony. But, apart from the general obscurity of these doctrines, it would surely be more plausible to suppose that, in whatever way a referent is involved, there must be different referents for radically different processes, most of all if the referent is continuous with the processes involved.

There is one consequence of the adoption of any version of the identity thesis which is very hard to avoid, namely that the efficacy of mental processes is at once put in jeopardy, however much some advocates of the thesis deny this, as in the case of Feigl. For, if our bodily states and our mental states are identical, it is hard to see how the course of our lives could be other than is required by the physical determination of the body.[5] What happens to me could, in principle, be known and predicted entirely from adequate knowledge of my body and the factors in my physical surroundings which impinge upon it. This does not mean merely that freedom of choice in some absolute sense, if that were being defended as I for one would wish to do, is out of the question, but that all our purposing is illusory. This runs completely contrary to all that we normally assume. When I rise from my seat and move across the room to open a window, the decisive factor here seems to be my own wish and intention to open the window (because I need more air perhaps, or in response to a request). But, on the identity thesis, the movements of my limbs would have come about in any case. All would have happened whatever I thought. This makes nonsense of all that we normally suppose. We exhort people to do things, we explain matters to them as required, and we assume that, if they understand, this will make a difference to what happens. If my wife calls and I go downstairs, this is because I understand that dinner is ready, etc., and surely my understanding counts, short of treating all purposive activity as some curious sort of reflex action.

Admittedly, I could not understand unless my brain were functioning properly (at least in the conditions we know in this world), nor could I hear my wife's voice if my ears were at fault, etc. But hearing the sounds and understanding what they mean counts also, and counts decisively where appreciating what it is like to lead a human life is concerned. Almost everything we think about ourselves, and all that we hold most precious, has to go by the board on a consistent acceptance of an identity thesis. Life would be one colossal illusion. I do not see how the identity thesis can escape this astonishing implication.

The question arises also as to what conceivable reason there could be for supposing that processes of the body and its brain are an eventually closed system open to no impact beyond itself. The style of the arguments adduced in reply is purportedly a scientific one. To be strictly scientific we must heed closely the correlations of processes in the brain and states of mind. But no one denies the correlation – the interaction thesis requires it; all that is questioned is the exhaustiveness of it. If it could be shown that changes in the brain continue in all respects as they would if subject to no influence 'outside' the body, then all would certainly be over with our normal assumptions and any case for inter-action. But why should we expect that or suppose that proper scientific study of the brain at its own level precludes the recognition that the impact of our thoughts upon it alters considerably what would have happened otherwise? Smart and Feigl concede this for the present state of our knowledge. We do not know enough *now* to prove conclusi-vely that the changes in our brains and our bodies generally continue unbroken by their own laws or momentum. They just assume, since science is so fundamental, that one day all this will come about. We can observe or record what goes on in the brain with sufficient completeness to be cer-tain that the story is fully told in those terms. Nothing will deviate from the course the physiological explanation would take; there will be no disconcerting gap in our record to require the postulation of something beyond it. But this prospect is admittedly remote – Feigl puts it at a thousand years hence—and why should we ever go in expectation of its being realised? Our common experience suggests quite the opposite and why should that be suspect on the remote off-chance that some day investigation of the brain will prove that we have all been living under a colossal delusion?

Some writers suppose that the onus of providing appro-priate scientific evidence at this point lies on the dualist. Thus Mr Keith Campbell writes:

Interaction of spirit and brain is not positively excluded by contemporary knowledge. Yet for most people researching brain function, the working hypothesis is that no such thing occurs. For in the absence of evidence to the contrary, the most economical and therefore best assumption is that only physical causes are at work. The interactionist dualist must bet that the economical assumption will prove inadequate to the facts. Until there is some sign of inadequacy, his bet is a baseless one, and hence one that in sound philosophy ought not to be made.[6]

But why should the dualist be put at such a disadvantage? He does not rest his case on special knowledge of the brain, indeed in strictness not on knowledge of the brain at all. His claim is that we do have experiences and purpose accordingly, and that what we purpose does in fact come about in the world with remarkable consistency that enables us to plan our activities within the conditions we have come to know; and why should he suppose, in the absence of such fantastic knowledge of the brain as may, or may not, prove it to be a closed system, that the implication of common experience is wholly mistaken and the seeming fulfilment of our purposes in the world just an enormous over-all fluke? The onus seems in fact wholly on the other side to provide evidence for what is, on all other counts, a most exceptionally improbable hypothesis.

It will help at this point to refer to a notion which is made central to a very important but somewhat neglected work, namely Nicolai Hartmann's *Ethics*, Vol. III. Hartmann draws attention to what he calls 'a plus of determination'. What he means is that there are different levels of determination, one being sometimes superimposed on the other without suspending it at its own level. Chemical determination may thus be taken up into organic determination, and the latter may be taken up into biological process. Properly human activity supervenes upon the latter, and within human life there are lower and higher levels related in the same way, including an area of free and wholly responsible choice. Each determination is strict at its own level, and there can be proper scientific study where appropriate. Chemistry is chemistry whether it has to do with stones or with plants or human bodies. But in the two earlier cases a different process takes the first into itself and makes a difference. In the same way purposive activity, while it does not suspend the activities that go on in the brain and the rest of the body, modifies the course of behaviour in certain ways and makes a difference to what would otherwise happen; it adds its own 'plus of determination'. I sometimes illustrate this in a homely way of my own by thinking of a number of people playing push-ball. Another player joins them. He cannot have everything his own way, the others are pushing already and the ball is being propelled in a certain direction, but his pushing makes a difference to the speed and direction in which the ball now moves. It is in the same way that mental processes supervene upon physical ones and make a difference to the outcome, just as they are themselves conditioned but not wholly determined by physical processes. We learn from experience in what ways such intervention is likely to be effective.

The reference to processes other than properly human ones brings us to a further, but substantially different, sort of objection sometimes brought against dualism. This involves a reference to what Professor Hirst calls 'the world in general'.[7] It is pointed out that there is a continuity in the life of sub-human creatures and ourselves such that it would be very implausible to tell one story in one case and a wholly different one in the other. In brief, we have to ascribe intelligence of some kind to brutes, and would we not then have to talk in dualist terms of their activities as well? I do not think anyone can seriously question the basis of this argument. The oddity is that anyone should have thought that a purely physical or mechanistic account could be given of the lives of brutes. The higher animals are clearly exercising intelligence very like our own in some ways. A dog penning sheep shows marked intelligence. How all this differs from our kind of understanding, and why it stops where it does, is a considerable problem, and we need not stop here to consider it. We can readily concede the principle of the continuity which Hirst has in mind. Dogs and horses, worms and insects, and even creatures much lower down the scale, have some kind of experience, and the higher animals have perceptual experience which must closely resemble our own. They recognise objects as we do, they dodge an obstacle in their path as we do, they are sensitive and attracted or repelled by one another, and they become very fond of some of us.

None of this need be questioned for a moment, and if Descartes himself did question it, that was more a concession to the prevailing views about the material world in his day. But what follows? The suggestion is that, while there might be some case for speaking, in sharply contrasting terms, of mind and body, or soul and body, in the case of human beings, it would be absurd to do this in the case of other animals; and if this is the case, the continuity in principle of intelligence in human and sub-human beings makes it very odd to insist on a sharp distinction in one case which we do not allow in the other. This has seemed to many a powerful argument. But the answer is simple. We have to draw the same distinction in the case of all animals down to the lowest sentient being on the scale, whatever that might be. This does not mean that we should speak of the *soul* of a dog. The idea of the soul could have further connotations, including appreciation of worth and a responsiveness to persons which require our kind of rationality. But the dog has his 'inner' life, the process of experience which goes on in a way of which he is aware but which cannot be directly observed. A reductionist or strictly behaviourist account of a dog in pain is as implausible as a similar account of ourselves. His pain is not his yelping or holding up his paw, nor any mere set of dispositions to do this. It is what he feels, just as all his perceptual experience is not wholly behaviour, but seeing and touching – as for us. The dualist does his case a grave injustice if he denies this. His case stands or falls with its being true all along the scale. My dog does not know that he likes being scratched because he finds himself wagging his tail and licking my hand. He *likes* it.

We arrive then at the view that mental processes, of whatever sort and at whatever level, are recognised in themselves to be of a radically different nature from extended or physical reality. There is a close interaction of mind and body in the case of animal life; and in this, with the extension to the case of brutes, Descartes seems to be entirely vindicated, notwithstanding such doubts as we may have about other aspects of his view. But it is also held that the distinctive mental processes we thus contrast with bodily states belong to or in some fashion characterise a continuing entity. Not all who concede the first claim will go with us in this further contention; and even if it is conceded that my experience at the moment belongs to me, or is had by me, as a distinct being, how do we know that the experience of half an hour ago and of yesterday and last year and my infancy are had by the same being who has the experience I enjoy now? How do we establish a continuing identity, and what is implied in doing so? It is to these questions that we must now turn.

5 Identity and Memory

The way we normally identify persons other than ourselves is through their bodies. My wife has just brought me a cup of tea. I know it was her because I saw her. My friend Brown has called, and I know that I am talking to Brown because I see him sitting in the chair. I may, on a very remote chance in these cases, be mistaken. If I was very deep in my work and did not look round I may not have noticed that my wife had sent the daily help up with the tea. Or my wife and Brown could have been impersonated by someone playing a trick on me. It would need indeed to be an almost unbelievably clever impersonation in these instances of persons I know so well. No one would be troubled by such a possibility. If I had looked and thought I saw my wife then I am sure that it was her.

Evidence of this sort is normally taken to be quite conclusive in some matters of grave importance. Suppose I hear X say something libellous about Y. Perhaps other persons present heard this also. In the absence of any reason to suspect the integrity of the witnesses (we have no motive for framing X or doing him harm) the court would take it as established that X said the words attributed to him. He might offer various defences. He might say that the words were spoken in jest, that he did not mean them as they were taken, that he was greatly provoked, etc. But one thing he would be most unlikely to say, if he expects to be taken seriously, is that he did not utter the words in question or was not present. To try the latter defence he would need to establish a very strong alibi and some very convincing evidence about someone who might impersonate him.

In other cases the issue is not clear. I may report that I saw X running from the scene of a crime. But then it was dusk and by the time a skilful counsel has finished with me

I may say: 'It looked so to me but I am not quite certain.' In some instances there may have been a long interval between the time a person was seen and his being confronted by those who are to identify him now. Suppose someone returns after thirty years abroad to claim a legacy. He will have changed much, especially if he left when he was young. He would need documents, evidence of people who have known him continuously or in good succession, etc., before we conceded his claim. But once we are convinced that the body which left the dock at London thirty years ago is the body, however changed, which is before us now, we have no doubt that we are confronted with the same person. Any doubts that remain concern the reliability of the evidence for the alleged bodily continuity. If the body has some mark which could not possibly be faked that settles the matter. If fingerprints had been taken we are content. What does this prove? Not nearly as much, for philosophy, as is sometimes supposed. No one denies, as has been much stressed already, that we live in our present existence in close dependence on our bodies and function through them; and, in whatever sense we come to think of ourselves as continuous beings, we find that this in practice is closely bound up with bodily continuity. The latter continuity is a perfectly reliable criterion of personal identity in all normal situations. But this in itself does not tell us in what the identity of the person himself consists, nor what reasons we have for believing in it. All that is shown is that bodily continuity can normally be taken to be a perfectly good guarantee of personal identity. In what does this identity itself consist, and has bodily continuity some place in it other than serving as a normal criterion?

Two answers suggest themselves here. One arises readily from the way we normally identify things. There is no absolute identity in the external world. We may draw the edges of things in a number of ways, according to the patterns and unities we find relevant for various purposes. This process is not wholly arbitrary, for if we were living in a wholly chaotic 'world', where things happened at random, we could not fix on anything as any particular entity. Happily there is a system in the world as apprehended in perceptual experience, and within the changes we note there is also a permanence or stability on the basis of which we manipulate objects and specify them. I thus regard the table as an entity, and likewise this or that book upon it. But the table has legs and a top, and the top has many leaves which could again be divided into many parts, indeed *ad infinitum*. The book has many pages, or in an alternative mode of division chapters, paragraphs, sentences, words, letters. Books may again, to move in the other direction, be part of a shelf of books in an alcove in a library, and the table is part of the furniture of one room which is part of a house in a village, in a country, etc. Whether we take the table as a unit, or the room or the house or the village, depends on what we are doing. If I am writing about villages in Surrey, or collecting statistics about villages, the unit is the village. If I am showing my guests where they are to sleep the unit is one room. If I am thinking about furniture the unit is the table, but if one leg of the table is damaged, the unit is the leg of the table, or maybe a defective castor or missing screw. The classifications are extremely varied, determined in part by the way things are in the world around us or the unities in our perceptual experience and in part by convention guided by our purposes.

The alternative to some view of this kind, (and we do not need for our purpose to spell out in detail what this kind of identification involves) is to suppose, as Locke did, that various qualities inhere in some quite unknown substance which is not perceived at all. But many have pointed out, with Berkeley, that we have no reason to suppose that there are substances of this kind, we have no experience of them as such, and they seem to explain nothing. We seem therefore left with the recognition of entities as this is dictated by our actual experience and the purposes we have in considering the world as we find it.

This is why it is sometimes notoriously difficult to determine whether some object has really remained the same or changed so completely as to be another thing. We have the well-known case of the bridge (or the suit of clothes) which has been so much repaired that none of the original material remains. Stone after stone has been replaced, and none of the original stones are left, though the general appearance is much the same. Or suppose the bridge is taken down, and a different one built in just the same place. We have now, in one obvious sense a new bridge, but we may not in fact give it a new name. For most practical purposes it is the same. You direct travellers to it in the same way. Most of Telford's bridge over the Menai Straits was removed a few years ago, but we still call it the Menai Bridge. The old picturesque Conway Bridge has been left in position, because it is so decorative, and a new one set up just beside it. We speak indifferently of both most of the time as the Conway Bridge. If we wished to compare the old with the new, in respect of beauty or convenience, we might distinguish sharply between them. But for other purposes we think of just the one bridge at Conway. There is thus nothing final or irrevocable, nothing which makes one unit in all circumstances the one we recognise, in our normal process of parcelling things out and identifying them.

Does this apply to minds? According to some thinkers it certainly does. There is only one principle of identity, however various the manifestations of it, and that is the one we have indicated as the mode of our identification of external things. We must, therefore, look for identity in human experiences in the patterns, the unity and continuity of them. I am the same person as I was half an hour ago because of a peculiar inter-relatedness of the experiences I had then and those I have now. This in turn is understood in various ways. According to Hume we have nothing but

> . . . a quality we attribute to our perceptions because of the union of their ideas in the imagination, when we reflect upon them . . . Our notions of personal identity proceed entirely from the smooth and uninterrupted progress of the thought along a train of connected ideas.[1]

But Hume himself was very conscious of the inadequacy of this account, he has no explanation of how 'the bundle or collection of different impressions' are held together. There is no 'principle of connection' and Hume very frankly confesses himself baffled, for on his theory there is nothing that could 'unite our successive perceptions in our thought or consciousness', he 'cannot discover any theory which gives me satisfaction on this head' and must simply 'plead the privilege of a sceptic'. Others ease the problem for themselves by looking to a unity of content and purposive activity. But this is very chancy if we are hoping to establish any firm identity of persons. For such unity flows out from one person's thoughts and experience to those of others, and in some cases it could leave the identity of a person at different stages of his life a very slender one. These are consequences which some thinkers are fully prepared to accept. There is not, on their view, anything peculiarly sacred about individual identity. It merges into the greater collective identity of groups or societies; and we have seen already how well this idea takes its place in the work of idealist philosophers of the late nineteenth century. Bosanquet, in addition, admits that identity becomes weak from one period of our lives to another when we may have undergone considerable change and that, for this reason, punishment, or at least the full measure of it, may not be appropriate after long lapses of time.

In the face of this and related difficulties, some are inclined to fall back on the idea of bodily identity as not merely the clue we normally adopt from day to day, but also as the substance of personal identity. The latter would then involve no more than the association, as cause and medium for effective purposing, of a set of experiences with a particular body. On a strictly materialistic view of persons this would seem inevitable, but it is hardly plausible on any other view. The identity theses which accord some place, as most of them do, to 'raw feels' or some other 'internal' or private factor, notwithstanding that it is ultimately held to be physical, will need to take some account of 'mental predicates' in any view they offer of our continued identity. If there is soundness in the view for which I myself have been arguing, namely that mental processes are radically different in nature from physical ones, and especially if I am right in my view that what is most distinctive of us as human beings is our mental life, it would be odd indeed to look for our identity or abiding character solely in the association with a continuous body, however that is conceived. Indeed, some have pointed out that the continuity of the body, as the body of an animate and rational being, can hardly be itself made intelligible in disregard of the mind which does so animate it. I shall not pursue that point here. For what seems most evident to me is that when we think of persons having a continuous history (and this is presupposed in all our normal dealings with one another), we are thinking primarily of attitudes of mind and various activities of ourselves chiefly as mental beings. The characteristic attitudes of personal relationships seem clearly to involve this.

Suppose that I said that I greatly admired someone, Mr Brown let us say again. Then this will be because I believe that he has done, or is inclined to do, certain things which are worthy of admiration — he is kind-hearted perhaps and is known to have helped many people in unobtrusive ways, or he is known to have endured grave misfortunes or ill-health with fortitude, or he is a gifted poet or philosopher. He may not be engaged in any of these ways at the moment. He is just sitting here smoking and probably thinking of nothing in particular. But he is also the person who did these things at various times in the past, and if I admire him now for what he has done in the past, and is inclined to do as occasion arises, this must surely be because there is some very vital link between him as a conscious being now and the various mental activites involved in the previous achievements in the past. If nothing were involved besides the accident of bodily continuity, most of our lives and affections would lose their point. We are indeed attracted to persons, usually of the opposite sex, because they have comely bodies. But even here, without going as far as Plato's view that the beauty of human form is wholly a reflection of the beauty of mind, we do not, except in cases of extreme infatuation (and perhaps not then), feel this attraction in a sustained and serious way regardless of qualities of mind. We like people because of what they are in non-physical ways, and sometimes in defiance of some physical defect. We hate someone because of what he did, that is, what he purposed or intended on some occasion, and hardly any of this would sensibly survive if we thought that there was no link between the person's present mental state and the dastardly action in the past other than a dependence in both cases on the same body. If we are not continuous at various times in our lives in some sense other than merely bodily continuity, then most that normally makes up the supposedly rich texture of human life, in day to day encounter as in art and literature, is hopelessly trivialised.

To what feature of mental life can we turn then for the properly mental component in self-identity? The idea which most obviously suggests itself here is that of memory; and most of those who have tackled the problem of personal identity have accorded a place of importance, in what they say, to memory. But to be clear we must first distinguish two senses in which we may use the words 'to remember'. I may say that I remember the date of the battle of Hastings or that Napoleon was defeated at Waterloo, or I may remember a poem. But all this means is that I can recall, as required, these items of information, or recite the poem. I do not remember the battle of Waterloo (and would not even if I were an authority on how it was fought) in the sense in which Wellington would have remembered it. He was *there*. And so we have a second meaning of 'remember' in which it is implied that if I remember something I was there, as actor or observer in some way. This can be interpreted narrowly or widely. I remember in a very precise sense having my breakfast this morning; I consumed it myself. I can also say that I remember the Battle of Britain. But I did not take part in this battle. What I remember strictly is reading about it at the time, hearing the news, being worried, distressed, relieved, etc. and all that went on in my own experience in consequence of knowing all the rest. But this makes no difference of substance to our discussion. What matters for us is that, if I remember in the second main sense, then I was in some way present myself in the events which I now recall – as in the simple case of having my breakfast or remembering drinking my tea a few minutes ago. If the words 'to remember' are used properly in the second main sense, then for me to remember something, if it ever happens that way, means that I .who remember now was also present or involved in some express way in the event I remember – 'means' in the sense that this is part of the meaning of the verb 'to remember'.

Now if we take remember in the first sense, in which I can quite properly say that I remember the date of the Battle of Hastings, this is not without importance for the problem of self-identity. It was indeed the central issue in Kant's notable treatment of the subject, and in those of many of Kant's followers. For if I do remember this date, that cannot be an isolated item in my experience, coming right out of the blue into my consciousness at some time. Memory is perhaps mysterious, but not in that way. The idea of the date is an elaborate piece of understanding, I can give it no meaning except in relation to other dates and my knowledge of a network of other events before and after it. I 'transcend' the present in all such acts of memory, whether of remote or of recent events. If I lived solely in the moment, I could hardly give meaning to anything. The only possibility would be that one experience by sheer association, or influence of that kind, set up or affected another; and, if anyone supposes that the vast network of our meaningful experiences can be accounted for entirely in that way, I strongly recommend to him to read carefully the masterly classical criticism of this notion in F. H. Bradley's chapter on 'The Theory of Association of Ideas' in Volume I of his most unhappily neglected *The Principles of Logic*[2].

Even in the case of brutes the theory of association is hardly plausible, though it has often been thought unexceptionable in respect to their more limited consciousness. My dog recognises me when I approach; he runs to greet me and lick my hand. If a stranger approaches he gets a very different 'welcome'. But it appears very strained to suppose that all that happens here is that different images spring up in the dog's consciousness. As H. H. Price has shown so well, there is recognition in some much more radical sense than that, and here again we draw too rigid a demarcation between brute and human consciousness at our peril. But keeping primarily to human consciousness, the meaningful experiences we normally have seem of themselves enough to establish at least some measure of abidingness from one

stage to another. Otherwise we have to suppose some
wholly mysterious instantaneous filling of our minds with a
very elaborate content involving a great deal in the past.
This does not mean that we must ourselves have lived
through all that we remember in the present sense. I did not
live through the Battle of Hastings, but, to know what reference to that battle means, I must have been the same
person through much experience during which I acquired
that understanding. But this still does not give us all that
we are on the track of now, namely just what it is that per-
sists through admittedly changing experience, and how this
is known – beyond the demand for something more actual
than an 'imaginary focus' as considered earlier.

To deal with this question account must be taken of the
second and stricter meaning of the verb 'to remember'. But
before I do that I must also refer to a further way in which
we may think of identity and thus come to the second of the
answers mentioned to the question of what our own identity
involves. We have seen that normally we identify things by
locating or describing them in some way. Unless I can say
something to indicate to what I am referring, my thought
seems vacuous. You have no idea what I am talking about;
neither have I myself. I must in some measure, however
general, say what it is to which I am referring, and this
means some kind of description. This seems unavoidable,
but is it so always? I do not think so. It does not hold, as
indicated earlier, of our initial idea of God. But then the
idea of God is peculiar. It falls outside the finite scheme of
things. Persons are finite, and they are known not obliquely
but, in essentials, for what they really are. Even so it seems
to me that there is one case where a person is identified
without any description to indicate what is intended, and
that is when each person identifies himself *to himself*. Each
one, I submit, knows himself in being himself, just as we all
know what thoughts and feelings we have, however we may
misdescribe them, in having them. This position comes very
close to that of Professor Shoemaker when he claims, in his
book *Self-Knowledge and Self-Identity*, that there is no criterion
of self-identity, at least in the sense in which a person identifies himself. But in presenting this view Shoemaker makes

a reference to our use of the verb 'to remember' which I do not accept at all points and to which I shall refer very shortly. In the meantime the contention is that a person does not need to show, in the basic sense, why or how he knows who he is. To ask this of him has an air of absurdity. He knows who he is – himself. He could be no other; nor is this in any way a verbal matter. We can none of us fail to know ourselves as the beings we are. There is a finality about the basic awareness that everyone has of himself.

This however needs some further explication. For there is certainly one very obvious sense in which a person may not know who he is. He may have lost his memory or be suffering from split-personality. These cases are not the same at all points. But they both present situations in which we might say that someone is not certain who he is. But the uncertainty only holds at a particular level. If I have lost my memory I have lost count of many things I normally know quite well about myself – and other people. I do not remember my name or where I live or what my work is supposed to be, etc. This is a terrible plight and has in it the seeds of great tragedy, as many works of fiction show. But there remains, all the same, a sense in which I am aware that this dreadful thing has happened to *me*. It is I who am suffering in this way, and the things I have really forgotten are peculiarities of my life and character. In being in this plight I know myself still as the one being I in fact find myself to be. Likewise, if a person is sometimes Dr Jekyll and sometimes Mr Hyde and has in one case no knowledge of the other, he nonetheless knows himself in all these changes as just the one being he knows himself to be. He is sometimes kind, sometimes cruel, but he knows himself as the kind or cruel person as the case may be. We are, in fact, all subject in some measure to changes or afflictions of this kind, and we forget much about ourselves, though without the complications of the conditions we consider to be pathological. But everyone knows in every situation, I submit, that he is the one being he finds himself to be.

To be more explicit, it will be well to distinguish here two major senses in which we may speak of a person's identity. One follows the way we think of the identity of other things.

It ascribes to them characteristics and a history. A certain person has a name, he was born on a certain day, he is married and has children, he works in a factory, he is kind-hearted, good-looking, is fond of football and usually smokes a pipe. The picture can be filled out more and more, and when it is fairly full we think we know the person well. This is especially so if we actually meet him and know what he looks like and what his gestures and facial expressions are, and know his habits and reactions closely. We can identify ourselves in the same way, building up as it were a picture of ourselves on the basis of what has happened to us and what we have done or felt. Such understanding is imperfect and sometimes quite wrong. We have often been urged to try to correct our picture of ourselves – to know ourselves or to see ourselves through the eyes of others, 'as others see us'. We have some advantages over other people in seeking to know ourselves in this way, and some disadvantages. We have more first-hand knowledge of ourselves in some ways, but we are also more biased, as a rule. But the point at the moment is that, however important self-understanding of this kind may be, it is a case of knowing better either certain facts of our own history or certain features of our characters. It does not indicate what it is for this particular history to be mine or these tendencies to be traits of *my* character. *I* am the person of whom all this is true, and in the case of personal identity the *I* is not any feature of what is known in this way, or a completion of it. There is a radically different sense in which I know myself to be this *I* that I am whatever the particular story which I (or someone else) tell about me. Irrespective of what I feel or think, I am the being I am, and would be if the story were different. This is what I call the basic sense of identity in which everyone knows who he is however little he may say about it or reflect upon it.

Normally, people do not reflect on matters of this kind, and it needs some degree of sophistication or philosophical competence to do so. But this does not mean that they do not have the awareness in question. It seems to me impossible for anyone not to have it, though it is easily possible, here as in other matters, for the issue to be obscured and to be questioned by those who do reflect.

Two further points will help at this stage. In saying that a certain thought or sensation is mine, in what I have called the basic sense of identity, it is clearly implied that thoughts, etc. 'belong' in some way to persons. But we have to be very cautious here. For we can have a very misleading model of what this belonging involves. We usually think of something belonging, either in the sense hardly relevant here of someone having a right (legal or moral) to it, or of a relation between distinct things or properties. This page belongs to this book, that is it is related to other pages in the book in some way. But it would be wrong to think of my thoughts or other experiences being attached or related in some similar way to me or my mind. The situation is in fact quite peculiar and without a strict parallel; and we go astray in looking for parallels. I am more than my thoughts at any particular time, not in the sense of other thoughts and experiences I have had, or any pattern or dispositional system these involve, but as the entity who has these thoughts here and now. But I cannot be characterised as such an entity, and my thoughts do not belong in the sense in which one thing belongs to another. My thoughts are mine in the very special sense in which thoughts are *had*. They are uniquely mine, though others may have thoughts like them, but what is meant by their being mine cannot be indicated other than in the way familiar to all in which we do have thoughts and sensations which could, nonetheless, have been different though I remained at the time the same being having them.

The complicating factor here, as in the case of recognising mental processes to be distinct from physical ones, is that we are unduly prone to *look* for the reality in question in some way akin to observing and noting what we find in the world around us. We do not find the self by looking or picking it out from other things[3]. It was Hume's mistake to suppose that it had to be this or nothing. We know ourselves, on the contrary, in the way each one finds himself to be the unique irreducible being he finds himself to be and having the thoughts, feelings, sensations, etc. he actually does have at any particular time. It is for these reasons that

the problem is a peculiarly difficult one to handle philo-
sophically. There is so much to say to avoid confusion and
wrongful expectation and, on the other hand, so little to say
beyond indicating what in fact we find to be the case.

It might be urged however, at this point, that, granted
that an experience of any kind involves a genuine subject
that has that experience, we still have no way of linking the
subject of any particular experience with those that have
gone before other than the general requirement that the
kind of experience I have now presupposes, or at least
strongly suggests as the most plausible explanation of it, the
kind of history in which I acquired my present accomplishments and understanding. That is in itself by no means
inconsiderable, as has been stressed; but we can, in fact, go
a good deal further, and this is the second of the two points
I have just mentioned. It concerns memory in the stricter of
the two senses indicated. Let me note first the way Professor Shoemaker, drawing on a very influential paper by
Professor Bernard Williams[4], presents the point in question
now. He observes that for a person to remember in the strict
sense implies that he was directly involved in the situation
remembered. To take a very simple example, if I remember
shutting the door then there can be no question about my
shutting the door – I must have done it. 'To remember'
means this, and thus we can argue from the meaning of the
verb 'to remember' that I must be now the person who also
did something else in the past. To this the reply may be
made that memory is fallible, we sometimes think we
remember when we do not – or we misremember. This
objection could take two forms, one of which would not
affect Shoemaker's position as seriously as the other. It
could be said that when I seem to remember seeing Brown
running from the scene of the crime in the dusk, it was not
Brown in fact that I saw – my eyes, as we say, deceived me.
But this is not strictly a fault of memory, but of my perceptual experience at the time. I may, however, think that I
remember something which I did not witness at all or
which I have in fact forgotten. This seems to happen to
some events in our early childhood about which we have
heard so often that we have the mistaken impression that

we in fact remember them. Can we then ever be quite certain that we do remember?

Shoemaker answers that, while we may not be altogether certain in every case, there must be very many cases in which we do remember in the strict sense. He supports this by arguments which do not seem to me adequate. He observes, for example, that we would not have a use for the verb 'to remember' unless there were some genuine instances of it. This seems to be a very question-begging appeal to language, not very far removed from the now notorious argument from the paradigm case. People speak of seeing ghosts or fairies, but we would need much more than that to convince us of the existence of either. Likewise, it would hardly be an adequate reply to Hume, when he takes up his sceptical view about the self, to say that we all refer to ourselves or to other persons; for the real question is what does this reference involve. To account for the sense that one has of oneself in terms of some association or similar relation of ideas may be extremely implausible, but it cannot be ruled out from the start by the short and simple method of just noting that we all do refer to ourselves. Shoemaker makes much also of the confidence with which we make memory claims. 'No one', he maintains, 'can have confident memory beliefs and at the same time hold that, for all he knows, most of them may be false'[5]. But we would dismiss today many beliefs that have been very confidently held from time to time.

It is odd also that Shoemaker should use this very formal *a priori* way of establishing our continued identity and yet insist on an essential, and not merely contingent, involvement of a person with his body – and odder still that, in pursuance of this somewhat paradoxical line, he should again have much recourse to the idea of memory. His argument here starts with the fact that we have perceptual experience of objects in the world around us. We could not, he maintains locate or describe such objects without placing some reliance on our memories; and we could not place the required reliance on memory without checking up on it 'by considering the evidence that other persons could also examine'[6]. But this correlation is not possible without a 'point of view' made possible by our bodies. The most that this argument proves, it seems to me, is that in order to have our kind of perceptual experience, we must have our sort of bodies. It does not, as I have urged at more length else-where[7], rule out the possibility of experience co-ordinated in some different way.

In spite of this, and the questionable way in which Shoe-maker deploys his main ideas, he seems to me to be skirting around an important truth all the time. It is true, for exam-ple, that we make some memory claims with great confi-dence, and feel on reflection that the confidence is justified. But this avails us now, not because of our confidence as such, but because it is warranted by our reflection on what in fact we find memory to be. What is this? My own answer is that we seem, in fact, able to recall the substance of some-thing that has happened without any independent evidence of its so happening. I can now remember clearly opening the door a moment ago. I do not think I opened the door and walked through because I am here and could not very easily be here without walking in. I might reason in the latter way sometimes – 'I must have left my hat in the train, for that is where they found it.' But that is very different from saying 'I remember', and I do remember opening the door. Some speak of this as a harking back to a past event or, sometimes, 'intuiting' the past. This may be questiona-ble, for the past event is no more. Memory is not like a film played over or some other way in which we peer at or wit-ness a past event anew. The past is over, and this is why the idea of some strict harking back or direct memory is so hard to defend. But however we cope with this, and it is a topic that would take us very far afield to investigate properly on its own account, there seems to be some way in which we recapture or recreate the past for ourselves now with a cer-tainty that requires no independent confirmation. This should not be confused, as it often is, with the vivid memory images or 'pictures' which help our memories so much. The 'pictures' are not themselves the remembering, but rather the assurance and understanding we have of what occurred.

But now, if I am right in the substance of what I have just been maintaining, I submit that we shall also find that when I do strictly recall or 're-create' the past in this way, I recall it in its fullness in the sense of its including, not merely what happened but my own distinctive awareness of myself at the time. I recall myself in the past event as the being I now find myself to be; and this establishes the completest identity we could have of myself, as I know myself now, and myself in the past. This seems to me to be the most basic feature of our identity. But the most strict identity established in this way does not itself cover the whole of one's life; we are very far from remembering all that has happened to us. We do, however, have very good reasons for building up around the core, or the most explicit linkages of past and present self, the body of further knowledge of events which I have also good reason to presume to be parts of my history in the same way. I hear, or discover from some evidence, of certain things which are continuous with my past as remembered and involving the body which is continuous with my present body; and there seem therefore to be the strongest grounds for presuming that those events were experiences of mine in the same way as my present experience or the experience I directly remember. I know myself in this way to be now, in the strictest and most basic sense, the same as the boy who went to school on a day of which I have now no personal recollection.

This gives us also a subsidiary, but not unimportant, sense in which we may speak of someone as the same person. We all retain some continuity of aims and interests. Some stability is guaranteed for us by our dispositional set-up, our characters and our aptitudes. Otherwise all would be chaos and life as we know it impossible. In this respect some of us are much the same as we were a year ago; we have the same main interests and react on the whole in the same way. Others may change markedly. From being rather gloomy and lifeless a man may become cheerful, enterprising, the life and soul of the party – he may have a sudden religious conversion or, as also happens, lose entirely the faith by which he has been living. We say in these cases that so-and-so is 'a changed man', he is 'not the same', 'you would hardly recognise him'. Some of these changes are more drastic than others, and it is a moot point how far the change has to go before we say 'He is not the same person'. Even in extreme cases the change is not complete, the words 'the same person' are fairly loosely used and the convention varies. All of us change in some measure and over long periods. All of us are very different from ourselves as children. But these changes occur to the being who remains essentially the same being through all such changes, however drastic. If I changed from being a cheerful person to being a gloomy one, if I lost all interest in philosophy and took to business instead, this would have happened to *me*, and my friends would say, '*He* is not the same.' This could be understood in terms of an underlying continuity (or, for some, bodily continuity), but, if I am right in what I have been maintaining earlier, there is a much more radical sense in which I am now the same as the cheerful person in the past.

This holds also for cases of abnormality, like loss of memory or split-personality. We all forget some things, and there are some differences in the images that most of us present in various roles and situations. The stern disciplinarian of the classroom may be very gentle at home. But sometimes these changes become extreme and pathological. The loss of memory, though never, I believe, complete, is tragic; and Dr Jekyll may not have any knowledge of Mr Hyde. But we take it none the less that these dreadful things have happened to the same person. How do we know this in extreme cases? Partly as a presumption from bodily continuity. But this is much reinforced when Dr Jekyll and Mr Hyde have a great deal of rather specialised and private knowledge in common – like where they keep things at home and so on. We might question Mr Hyde about things which only Dr Jekyll could know. In that case various explanations would be possible. It could be that Jekyll and Hyde are two distinct persons who occupy the same body in turn, as is alleged in the celebrated case of Eve White and Eve Black. Varied explanations of this could then be given. We might suppose that Jekyll communicated something telepathically to Hyde, and if we allow telepathy it would be plausible to assume that it would be helped when two persons could be expected, by their alternate occupation of the same body, to be in some rapport – or psychically sympathetic. On the other hand, we might find our clue in the fact that the same brain is involved. This, in itself, makes the idea of alternate occupation of one body bristle with difficulties. The brain, in spite of the fact that different parts have different functions, is very much a whole organism – as indeed is the whole body. It is hard to suppose that one part becomes quite dormant while one tenant is 'in'. How does the transition take place without disruption? But we can leave this for the present. On the supposition that two persons are, in fact, involved we could suppose that the way the brain functions in respect of memory makes possible also the awareness by Hyde of something which only Jekyll could know (such as where he has concealed something) – the awareness is made possible by certain conditions of the brain which they somehow share. In that case it would not be memory in the strict sense. For Hyde cannot possibly remember what Jekyll did, if memory in the strict sense is of some situation in which a person is directly involved – we would have a quasi-memory. That is not, in my view, ruled out. On the other hand, the difficulties involved in the idea of alternate occupancy of the same body are so considerable that it seems much more likely, in the case of Jekyll and Hyde, that it is the same person who undergoes sudden changes of disposition and very drastic lapses of memory, due primarily, one supposes, to certain physical conditions. In that case we would say that Hyde did not know that he was also Jekyll, but that all the same, in spite of this total oblivion, he would in fact *be* Jekyll; and what I am most concerned to maintain at this point is that it is quite proper to suppose that this can happen, whether or not the evidence suggests that the oblivion is as complete as we imagine in a particular case. My view of the self does admit of continued identity in spite of the drastic changes envisaged.

In the measure, however, that there is some continuity of memory, the actual establishment of identity is firm in spite of drastic changes of another sort. This is what gives such point and strength to Locke's celebrated example[8] of the prince who wakes up to find himself in the body and outward circumstances of the cobbler. There are more difficulties in this supposition than is always realised, and I shall note them in a related context in a moment. But suppose that we give play to our fancy and suppose this remarkable transition established. The prince remembers all he would normally remember, that he was in his court the day before and went to his own bed last evening. Who then is he now, and who would the cobbler be if their circumstances had been reversed? Naturally everyone takes the prince to be the cobbler, and all expect him to behave accordingly. But he will know, and know beyond any dispute, that he is the prince – or the person who had the status and circumstances of the prince before. He will certainly know this if he has the prince's memories – if they are genuine memories. For he will not merely recall what happened to the prince but that it happened to him as the being he now knows himself to be.

This is closely in line with what we would normally say. If the prince had his usual memories, he would not hesitate to conclude that he was now, in spite of all outward change, the prince of yesterday. He might bemoan his fate, or rejoice in it and set out to exploit it. If it were a change for the worse – as we would normally assume in the case of the prince – he might protest very vigorously. If he were about to be whipped he might cry out, 'It wasn't me'; and if he could go on to tell us things which only the prince could be expected to know, but knew nothing of the things that would be familiar day by day to the cobbler, then we would also be convinced. For much the most likely explanation is that he would be remembering the things which it would be remarkable for the cobbler to know. But while many philosophers, like Shoemaker and Penelhum today, would concede this, they would not agree that it makes it possible to establish continued identity on the basis of memory alone.

This is because they would argue that memory claims require to be checked. In the case of Penelhum and Shoemaker, especially the latter, the admission is made that it is a necessary truth that memory claims are usually true. I am not happy about the linguistic reasons adduced for this, and have made that plain elsewhere[9]. But the point is that, although the admission is made, it is made in a form and context[10] which requires also the checking of particular memory claims and the establishing of identity in a way that involves, at least as one component, certain bodily observations. We could thus not establish our personal identity in a way that did not require the establishment of bodily identity as well. But it is not clear to me that this argument, even if the initial assumptions are allowed in full, establishes quite as much as is supposed by advocates of the identity thesis. The most that it might be thought to show would seem to be that bodily continuity must be the rule for most of us in this existence if the reliability of memory is to be made sufficiently firm to be a basis for self-identity. It would then be possible, once the general dependability of memory had been established in this way, to allow of its being trusted even in the absence or suspension of bodily continuity in particular cases, especially as the present way of confirming our confidence in memory does little to explain further how or why it operates. But what matters even more is that, even if bodily continuity were indispensable, in the way indicated, to establish our personal identity, this would still fall very far short of showing that the person whose continued identity was thus established was himself a physical being or had a strictly physical component. All we could be certain of would be that a physical condition was essential for us to be aware of our identity – or justified in believing in it.

If, however, I am right in contending that there is some kind of immediacy in memory which justifies our confidence in it, for the most part, then the case made, along the lines indicated, for an essential identity of mind and body falls to the ground. We need not, as I have already noted, suppose that memory is some strictly harking back to the past event or curious witnessing of some kind of replay. But there is a case for saying that in memory we do have an assurance on which we feel fully entitled to rely, as a rule, without independent confirmation. That is what remembering feels like. Nor is this directly bound up with the vividness of our memory images. Most of us have such images, but it is not clear that we rely on them equally in all cases. Indeed it could well be that we exaggerate the place of such images because, when we try to reflect on what it is like to remember, we are too readily disposed to fix upon the element in the total experience which is most easily described and identified. But whatever we say of this, the remembering itself is not the having of a mental picture or image; and once we realise this we may be better placed to appreciate that, however it operates and whatever further problems it presents, there is some way in which memory, without being infallible, guarantees itself. In that case it establishes an identity of a very special kind, since it includes the peculiar consciousness that each one has of himself at any time, independently of any direct dependence on bodily continuity.

Is not this the way we would think of the prince's awakening in the cobbler's bed? At first, perhaps, he is not fully awake, and then his dreaming state passes into more conscious reverie. But his eyes are still shut and the metamorphosis has not become apparent. He then clearly thinks of himself as the prince and he could well be recalling what he did the day before. He only becomes bewildered when he notices the room and the feel and appearance of his own body. But however upsetting that experience may be, he will surely go on thinking of himself as the person who went to bed as a prince, and he will not seriously doubt the clear and coherent memories he has of the day before and of other days. Even if he wonders for a moment whether he may not be dreaming he will soon be convinced that he is not; it is not a dream world that he inhabits. Even in dreams our memories could still be dependable, and some could be clear and coherent in themselves. The prince, in short, could trust his memories for what they are; and for that reason he will be quite certain who he is however changed in outward form and circumstance.

I have, however, been urging also that, even if memory fails us, and even if our dispositions and circumstances underwent a drastic change, we could still *be* the persons we were in previous events, though *ex hypothesi* we could not *know* this in the absence of some other more particular way of linking ourselves with those events. Indeed, there is much in the course of a person's life of which he retains no recollection and of which no explicit record is available. With effort I could presumably determine where I spent some particular day in the past, but unless I have kept a very careful diary I may not be able to ascertain much else about it. Did I go for a walk, did I stay in my study in the evening or visit friends? There may be no answer. But we do not for that reason doubt that I am the same person as the one who was engaged in these forgotten activities. For some thinkers this will be due to presumed bodily continuity, and in the absence of this and some evidence which has a physical component, it is hard to see how we could ever *know* that we are the persons involved in forgotten events. Paranormal assurance might perhaps do, and there may be substance in the view that we could, under certain conditions, be induced to remember all we have done – it is all 'stored' perhaps in the brain to become a live memory if appropriate conditions could trigger it; and psychiatrists, we are told, have some remarkable successes in inducing a recall of forgotten events. But even when this fails us, as normally happens, we do not doubt that personal identity remains unaffected, and what I am concerned to insist upon here is that even if we have no memory or other knowledge of a past experience, and could not therefore know of ourselves as the persons involved in it, that in no way precludes our *being* the subject of it. In terms of my own account of self-identity, I would have known myself, in the forgotten event, as the being I now know myself to be.

6 Reincarnation

The view I have just been defending is presupposed in much that is said about reincarnation. Some of those who believe in reincarnation maintain that they know 'what they were' in their past life – or have some similar memory. But if the doctrine is meant to apply to all of us, as is usually the case, and to all living things, then there seem to be instances of any number of people who have no recollection at all of their alleged previous existence – or any inclination to believe that they had one. But this does not in itself in the least rule out the possibility that they have 'lived before' and were, in the strictest sense, the persons they are now, notwithstanding great difference between their past life and the present one. On the score of its conceivability in the present sense, the doctrine of reincarnation has nothing to fear.

It does not follow that there are no other considerable difficulties. There are, and those who hold the doctrine are not often as ready as they should be to indicate how they would deal with them. One very obvious problem is this. Unless we suppose that the process happens in a wholly random way – and this would be quite at odds with the nature of Karma and of gaining merit in one life for the next – how does it come about that another appropriate life is ready when the time comes for the rebirth? We have to remember that much in our dispositional nature and skills is settled through conception and the transmission of physical characteristics. This need not mean that the whole course of one's life is predetermined; but clearly much of it is. We have 'gifts of nature' and 'gifts of fortune'. How, then, can a soul come to an appropriate new birth without suspension of the normal course of natural events? Is there a miraculous modification each time, and how would that square with available evidence? And what, moreover, can we say of changes in the population? On what principle can it be thought that new souls are created? Some easement may be found in the notion that one kind of existence need not be continued in its like the next time, the commonest supposition where the idea of rebirth is held. One may not come back the next time as a human being. But, even on this understanding, there seems to be required some very remarkable manipulation or pre-established harmony to ensure the appropriate new life as the principle requires.

A partial solution to these kinds of difficulties may be found by thinking of 'the cycle of rebirth', as is, in fact, usually done, against the background of aeons and aeons of time. If we suppose that the soul may have to wait a very long time for its next embodiment, it becomes a little less improbable that the appropriate new life and setting would be available. But even when the process is viewed in this very vast way, the required permutations of the dovetailing of appropriate lives into one another in life as we know it is dauntingly high. There remains the question also of the status of the soul in-between its embodiments. There is no insuperable difficulty here, provided the soul is credited, in the intervening state, with some kind of experience or activity. It could not, if I am right in what I have held earlier, just simply be or exist. But it could, in principle, exist in some other form than material embodiment. How far that consists with an acceptable notion of the way things must operate in the kind of system or universe envisaged in these beliefs is another matter. Would existence in some state of suspension between various embodiments be inferior or superior to the latter? On some views of a tenuous existence in the Shades, it would be very inferior, but not so when it is thought that release from a physical body would open out possibilities of a richer experience in some other form. The doctrine of Karma would perhaps be elastic enough to be made consistent with either possibility. There would also be the question of the purpose to be served by (or, as some would put it, the seeming pointlessness of) so much repetition of like experience from one life to the next. I should myself, in spite of having had a happy childhood, view with the greatest distaste the thought of starting all over again as a baby. But for the moment I shall not pursue these general considerations further. There are, however, two other points that can best be raised at this stage.

One of these concerns the limit of any metamorphosis we may be expected to undergo. On some doctrines of reincarnation, and even more in popular acceptance of it and in its mythology, there seems to be no limit. One might 'come back', at some stage at least, as almost anything. But when this is envisaged there is also a failure to take the idea of the transformation involved in its fullness. The change seems to be a change of form only, one has the body of a piglet and the consciousness of a man. This is hard to take seriously, although of course we can easily give our imaginations poetic licence to play with such a possibility for fable or other fiction – and presumably seriously at times, as in the case of those who take literally the Bible story of Nebuchad-nezzar being put out to grass. How the body and brain of a donkey could serve the embodied existence of a creature with human aptitudes and understanding seems to be beyond conceiving in terms of anything we know of such conditions. It looks then as if we would have to take the doc-trine in a more wholehearted way, and there is little doubt that this is the serious intention of it. If, to live out my Karma, I have to return as a brute I really become a brute. But could one's identity be thought to be continued in such a state?

If this supposition daunts us, it may be well, in fair-ness, to remind ourselves of the changes we have in fact undergone. We have all been babies, and we have all been in the womb. Presumably we would want to say that we were the same person then as now, at least from the moment of birth. This is easier, in some respects, for those who think of identity in terms of a pattern of change or of merely physical continuity. We can identify the body as the same body in the usual way through many changes in terms of continuity and patterns of change. The identity is partial and it is weakened when the change is drastic, and this is why, as I noted earlier, responsibility for a moral act becomes weaker, it is thought, after a long lapse of time and change of character. But if we take a less conventionalist or relativist view of the identity of persons, and if we firmly maintain, as I have been doing, that one remains strictly the same being in wide variations of state and circumstance, then one can maintain that one is strictly the same being as the very limited creature one was at birth. And why stop there? I certainly was not myself at conception, I did not exist then as a person. But at some point between this and birth (at the quickening?) I must have acquired some kind of sentience, and if we presume in other ways a continuity of personal existence where there is continuity of one's body, it would be hard to exclude from this our existence in the womb from the point, whatever it may be, when we have reason to suppose that more than a physical organism is involved.

But it is one thing for the kind of experience we would normally have to be reduced or attenuated in some way – this happens in any case in dreams or in states of semi-consciousness due to drugs or illness. It is quite another thing to have, in a full and positive way, the reactions and aptitudes of a quite different sort of creature. I might be reduced, in some condition, to the kind of experience, just having physical sensations perhaps, which I can share with a dog. But if I had in full the sensations, responses and dispositions of a dog, if I had not only its outward shape but its brain and nervous system and all that goes with that, then it certainly seems hard to suppose that, in so complete a metamorphosis as this, I could be the being I now know myself to be. Perhaps it would be going too far, on my presuppositions, to say that identity of the subject could not be conceived, or thought logically possible, in such changed conditions. But there is certainly much to be pondered in this context by those who maintain, in my view much too readily, that one's identity could be thought to persist in some way even when a human being becomes, as is alleged, a dog or a worm or an insect. The change in kind seems too complete here to allow an identity of being.

In that case it would seem also that we would need some limit at the upper end of the scale. Quite clearly a man could never become God; he would cease to be the finite being he is. But long before that aspiration is thought of, there must be limits to the metamorphosis possible to us. There may well be many modes of being besides the ones with which we are familiar, as creatures of time and space (as Spinoza implied in his doctrine of infinite attributes). We can form no conception of what they could be like. But that is no reason for questioning whether they are possible. In another existence, if we have one, we shall presumably be very much changed, not only in character but in the kind of existence we have as well. We expect indeed to be closer to God, redeemed and made whole in 'the general assembly and church of the first born', as the *Epistle to the Hebrews* has it. But we shall also have shed our present mortal flesh. There will presumably be some other way to particularise and order our experience, some kind of 'spiritual' body or a dream body perhaps. We shall need to recognise one another in some way. But we can certainly have very little discernment now of what this will be like; we can only have very tentative speculations, exciting though some of them may well be. The change will be drastic in some ways. But what I wish to note at the moment is that, although 'we know not what we shall be', there must be some limits to the kind of change in mode of existence which would be compatible with our being the creatures we find ourselves to be; and this has a bearing on the question, to which I shall return, of whether some kind of embodiment may not be indispensable.

We should not, on the other hand, underestimate the very vast extensions of experience and attainment that is in due course possible to us, in religion as in other regards, without any radical departure from the kind of rational creaturely existence we have now. For here again the possibilities seem to go far beyond anything of which we have any clear conspectus now – as the scientific attainments of our day go far beyond anything that was conceivable, except in the dimmest outline, to bygone ages.

I come now to the second of the two points which I said I would like to raise at this juncture. It concerns the sort of evidence which might be relevant to the claims made about reincarnation. The idea of reincarnation is not made to rest, as a rule, on particular evidence. The main line of defence is more *a priori* and metaphysical, consisting in part of views about our constitution as persons and in part, the essential part it would seem in serious reflection, of consideration of what certain alleged demands of justice in the universe as a whole, or 'in the nature of things', require. But some evidential support is also provided for the theory. This consists in part of the experience, not very uncommon, of a sense of familiarity with persons or places which it is unlikely, or outright impossible, for us to have known at any previous time in the present life. In some cases the experience appears to be a very compelling one and people have been known to swear in such cases that 'I know I must have been here before'. It does not seem, however, that very great weight can be attached to a feeling of this kind. For various explanations of it are possible, even when it is very strong and vivid. We may have had a dream where the shape of things, and the circumstances also perhaps, were very like what we are experiencing now – and the dream may have gone without trace. There may also be subtle combinations of things we have only vaguely observed from time to time, things in the margin of our attention of which we have not taken any proper note and which may blend in turn with the stuff of dreams and reveries. If the impression is too strong to admit of explanation in these terms (and at what point would that, in fact, be reached?), we can have recourse to various forms of paranormal influence for which claims are also often made. If we can consider pre-existence, we can presumably have an open mind about telepathy and clairvoyance. Perhaps we have had a subtle clairvoyant awareness in the past of the 'familiar' place we are visiting now, or an impression of it may have been communicated to us (or be communicated now?) telepathically by someone else. For these reasons, the impression of familiarity, even when pronounced, is hardly sufficient in itself, that is without further clear impressions or memories, to provide more than very slight or tentative support for so remarkable a view as that we have actually lived on this same earth before, perhaps many times.

It is another matter when, as is sometimes alleged, a

person has, not a vague sense of familiarity, but a distinct recollection of something that is supposed to have happened in a former life. The difficulty here again is that of assessing the soundness of such claims. I have maintained earlier that we generally trust our memories for just what they are for the most part; in some way they seem to validate themselves and give us assurance of something having happened in which we ourselves were involved. But I have also admitted that, hard though it may be for such a theory, we do, in fact, misremember. We cannot go against the facts, and it would be hard to present them as anything other than properly misremembering, though an ingenious person might try. The general claim is not, I think, wrecked on that score. But we do, all the same, have a different situation on our hands when we are faced with so remarkable a claim as that we have memories of a quite different existence.

This is not because such a claim can be ruled out in principle. Granted the conceivability of a former life, and that is not at issue at the moment, there is no inherent reason why we should not have some memories of it. Admittedly, what we can remember of our present life is largely conditioned by certain states of the brain. But if we allow the possibility of any other existence than the present one (future as well as past), we are setting a limit to the way our mental life is conditioned by the brain and body we have now. Whether memory as such, in distinction from other experiences, requires some kind of embodiment or condition by which it is sustained is a moot question. But if we conceive the possibility of a future or a past existence at all, it must be in terms of some radically different situation from that which normally obtains in our present life; and there seems to be no reason to suppose, in that case, that the conditions by which we are enabled to remember now are not superseded by some other conditions, or perhaps waived altogether, in circumstances that extend beyond our present life. There is of course a difference when such an extension concerns a previous life lived on this earth, or its like, in the same way as at present, and this seems to tell against, rather than in favour of, our having memories now of a previous life on earth. For in both cases we are functioning in substantially similar conditions of embodiment. A greater scope seems to be allowable in a more radically altered situation. For although a person has a brain, in his alleged previous life, very similar to his present brain, it is not the same brain or continuous with his earlier brain in a way which might be thought to carry some 'record' or effect of the events of the previous life. Such considerations do not however preclude a memory of a previous existence made possible in some other way than the normal functioning of brain and body in general in remembering. It is simply that, on the whole, remembrances of a like past existence is less probable than memories we may be thought to have in some completely different state of which we can have little understanding now.

Let us come back then to the main question of evidence. If we allow, as I have done, that memories are fallible or, to adhere to the strict meaning of memory as a way of being aware of what has in fact occurred, that we have seeming memories which appear to us at the time to have the mark of genuine ones, then we may well find much to make us hesitate over claims to remember a past existence even when we have no doubt of their sincerity. We generally feel more confident about memories of very recent events. There seems to be more, in the case of remoter events, to come between and cloud the issue. But perhaps remoteness does not count in a case which cuts right across normal conditions. Even so, as in the case of a feeling of familiarity, conflated impressions of various kinds, coming from various levels of waking or dreaming experience, could on some occasions come to seem like a genuine memory and take us in. Most of us have the experience of wondering, about some events, whether we really remember them or have been told about them so often and pictured them that we come to think that we remember them. This holds especially of events in the dim period of early childhood, but there are also cases, it appears, when people have come to believe firmly that occasions which they themselves invented or imagined in the first instance did really take place. The world of fantasy is very real for some and the edges become blurred between the world of fantasy and the real world. Since images play so important a part in remembering, it would be easy here also for the unwary to take the dream for the reality and suppose they have memories when this is not at all the case.

It follows that, while we would normally be inclined to take a sincere memory claim at its face value, we would require exceptionally clear evidence in respect to claims to remember a previous life. This would hold even in one's own case. For though it is hard for those who have not had such an experience to envisage quite how closely it would have the feel and firmness of a normal memory, it would presumably be cut off from ordinary sequences and be more open to possibilities of delusion. The gap between the events of the past life, as we seem to remember them, and our knowledge of the present life could only be closely filled by some very extraordinary paranormal form of awareness; and I am not aware that the claim is made to have sustained clairvoyant knowledge of the past in this way. The claim is confined to slices of the past through which we have lived ourselves and which we could, to that extent, be allowed to remember. It follows, in the light of these difficulties, that a claim to remember incidents of a past existence, or a continuous stretch of it, would require, even in one's own case, the support of overwhelming evidence. What form could this take?

It would have to take the form of someone being able to describe, in sufficiently impressive detail, certain events of a life lived in the past of which the narrator could not be expected to have knowledge in the normal way, but which could be verified by others. Let us suppose that someone claimed to know in detail how an otherwise unknown merchant in the Middle Ages spent his days. We are told where the merchant goes morning, noon and evening, to whom he talks and so on. Suppose that in addition a diary comes to light soon afterwards which coincides closely with the original account, descriptions of how people and places looked, how they arranged themselves at the table, what story this or that person told and so on. What would we say in this case? One's first reaction would be one of suspicion. 'Fraud', we would say; someone had discovered the diary first and, for some reason, had contrived to keep it secret until its contents had been divulged by the person who claimed to remember them. The latter would presumably be an accomplice, but we could also just suppose that he was innocent and had been cleverly fed the appropriate information, in some subliminal way perhaps. But suppose the circumstances tell heavily against the possibility of fraud; then we would have to consider seriously what other explanations could be given.

I have deliberately stressed the need for precise and significant detail. Otherwise it might be supposed that the story had been composed in the first place out of the information that is generally available about life in the Middle Ages, although there are, in fact, not many who have more than a very general knowledge of this. It would be remarkable for a person with average education and no special interest in history to compose a convincing narrative of life in the Middle Ages or some other remote period. But genius takes many forms, and novelists have been known to provide lively and convincing fiction about lands they have never visited. We could rule out any explanation along these lines however by supposing that the details of the narrative were too circumstantial to be the result of an exceptionally lively imagination making the most of the little information available. The story, we may also suppose, is told by a person not likely to have any proper knowledge of the period.

These conditions rule out a great deal that is popularly claimed in these contexts. A short while ago the papers gave much prominence to the claim of one gentleman to remember how he came to meet his death in the battle of Sedgemoor. But he had nothing to say about the battle that would not be readily available in any case; and the details of the way he came to be killed could not be confirmed independently. On the other hand, where the details tally closely and the possibility of fraud is ruled out, we have to take seriously the claim that certain events of a previous existence are being remembered.

I say, 'take seriously', for still other explanations are available. It could be that the person who has now discovered the diary conveyed the information telepathically to the narrator before anything was otherwise known of the discovery. This could happen without the source of the communication being disclosed. If, however, the narrator told his story before the discovery, we would have to allow of a very odd and, to my mind impossible, case of telepathy before the event – working backwards as it were. But the telepathic communication might have come from some other source – from people who had at some earlier stage handled the diary or the author of it or others who witnessed, or were told, of all it describes. This could have two forms, directly from the persons concerned at the time, or from themselves or others in contact with them who have survived and exist in some way now – but not 'on earth', for that would assume the theory for which we are seeking to canvass alternatives. Clairvoyance could also be invoked. The narrator could have a clairvoyant knowledge of the contents of the diary or some kindred paranormal awareness of the events it describes. We would need to consider these possibilities, and further variations on them, before we could firmly conclude that the narrator was in fact remembering events from a past life of his own.

I should add that, for my own part, I would be inclined to attach more weight to explanations in terms of pre-existence than to clairvoyance or telepathy, and would find the former hard to resist, notwithstanding all that one knows of the perils of credulity, if the circumstantial details were precise and sustained and the likelihood of fraud eliminable or remote. The main point however, at the moment, is that, if the doctrine of reincarnation is supposed to have evidential support, it needs to be presented and tested along such lines as those that have been indicated. This, in fact, rarely happens in the contexts where such claims are usually advanced.

A subsidiary problem presents itself here. It is also a problem that has attracted surprising attention among the more tough-minded philosophers whom one would not normally associate with intriguing speculation. The problem arises if we consider the possibility that more than one person should seem to have the memories of someone who is now dead. Suppose, in the stock example, two people (or more) appear to have the memories of Guy Fawkes. What then do we say? In terms of my inclination to agree that, if the memory claims tally closely with facts otherwise ascertained, and if we can rule out fraud, then the likelihood is that there is a genuine memory of a previous existence, we have a truly disconcerting situation on our hands. There seem to be living now two people both of whom we must consider to be identical with an earlier one. Has Guy Fawkes now become two persons? Can a person be divided in that way? One's firm inclination is to say 'No', and it is on the presumption that this sort of answer is unavoidable that many recent writers have concerned themselves with this sort of dilemma. For they conclude that there can be no solution short of making bodily identity at least a condition of personal identity. If we insist on bodily identity, then neither of the persons now claiming to be Guy Fawkes can really be so. But we have seen that there are strong reasons against making bodily identity a condition of personal identity and, unless we surrender all that has been said on this score earlier, the problem remains.

In any case, the reluctance we have to say that Guy Fawkes has now become two persons springs directly, it seems to me, from the conviction we have that personality is essentially incapable of being divided; and this conviction comes from our awareness of ourselves as unique beings incapable of being or becoming any other. If we could interpret this uniqueness in a less absolute way than I have maintained it to be, we might find the situation easier. For we could then take a relativist or conventionalist view of what constitutes a person. This would allow, as we have seen, of some merging of persons, as we find in idealist doctrines. The criteria of personal identity would be fluid, and it might then be possible to suppose that a person is, in some respects one, in some respects two. We would decide, with practical purposes in mind, when a person is one, and when he is two, and we might thus conclude that, while the pattern of the life and experience of the original Guy Fawkes sets him apart as a distinct person, the same criteria require us now to recognise two of him. But while procedures of this kind are open to many who take a different view of personal identity from the one which I favour, such recourse is not open to me. For I have maintained that personality, in the strict sense, is inherently incapable of being divided. There just cannot be two Guy Fawkes.

There remain then two possibilities. One, and that is the one we would, in my view, be most disposed to take, is to say firmly that the alleged memories of a life as Guy Fawkes can only be genuine in the case of one of the pretenders, if I may so call them. That is, we would say on *a priori* grounds that it is not possible for one person to be, or become, two. This we would say on the basis of what we know of being a person ourselves. And it seems to me clear that we should do this. There is therefore no possibility of looking round for meanings of personality which might make it easier to speak of Guy Fawkes now as one, now as two, though there are subsidiary meanings of personality which might admit this. What then of the alleged memories? The answer must be that, however convincing the claim may at first appear, in terms of the close tally of the 'memories' with the known facts, etc., only one set can be strictly memories. Perhaps neither are. But certainly not more than one. For only one person can have the memories of Guy Fawkes, that is Guy Fawkes himself; for memory involves, if I am right, recalling the events participated in by the unique being that everyone finds himself to be. We would thus conclude, in the situation envisaged now, that one set of 'memories' must be pseudo-memories. The owner of these has come to know, in some preter-natural way, of what went on in the life of Guy Fawkes and he may perhaps also visualise or image this in a way very similar to having memory images proper. He may be confused on that account in what he reports to us. But whatever the explanation might be, he cannot be having memories, in the strict sense, of the life of Guy Fawkes if someone else has them.

It may seem somewhat strained or far-fetched to suppose that a person has acquired by clairvoyance or telepathy (or some combination of these) a body of knowledge of what went on in the private life of someone now dead. But then the supposition that anyone can have such knowledge in any way other than the normal one, and that two persons might appear with substantial apparent memories of the same past life, is in any case an extraordinary one of which it is not easy to find possible examples for which a truly strong case could be made. All that I need to say at present is that, in the event of a convincing case being presented, we would have to suppose that the seeming memory must in one case be accountable in other terms than memory proper. That those would have to be very strange does not matter so much here, for the entire supposition in which the problem arises is in any case a strange one. We do not have to explain how everything would happen in a supposed situation which would certainly defy explanation in normal ways.

The second possibility is that Guy Fawkes has in fact come back to life again, not, as we have deemed to be impossible, as two persons, but as one person with two bodies. How remote then is this possibility? On the face of it we would be inclined to say that it is not possible at all. No one can be in two places at once, we say. This would be taken as axiomatic for most purposes in this world. A cast-iron alibi would depend upon it, and no law court would refuse to accept such an alibi. Suppose, for example, I were accused of committing a crime in Manchester some evening. I claim, however, that I was reading a paper to a learned society, the Aristotelian Society let us say, in London at the time. Many who attend the Aristotelian Society know me. We can hardly suppose that anyone who tried to impersonate me on such an occasion could get away with it. He would not only have to get himself to look exactly like me but to have my voice, demeanour and gestures, and also to know my paper and the line I would take in discussion of fairly abstruse topics sufficiently to take in professional colleagues who know me. Even allowing for changes of style and theme no one seriously supposes that sustained deception of my close acquaintances in this way is possible. A dummy might take them in if it had just to sit still, and a double might get away with a few minutes. But it would have to be shown that I had a double (unknown to my friends hitherto), and even he could hardly survive the discussion. In short, if my friends and others at the meeting swore in court that I was reading my paper to them that evening, this would certainly suffice to clear me; and this is on the firm assumption that, if I can be shown beyond reasonable doubt to have been at the meeting, it follows that whatever went on at Manchester, I could not have been there to commit any crime. Even if it is only reasonably possible that I was the one in London there would be sufficient doubt to aquit me. This is what we normally take to be beyond dispute.

But suppose now that someone were to say: 'We do not deny that you were at the London meeting, the evidence is quite conclusive on that. What we hold is that you were also in Manchester and that there you committed this terrible misdeed.' What would we say to this? Preposterous, impossible. Yes, perhaps, but it is worth asking at least why we are so firmly convinced that it is absurd to suppose that a person can be in two places at once. There are, in the first place, at least two ways in which this suggestion might be understood. I might be thought to be in some place other than the location of my present body if I were able to exercise causation at a distance. I might thus be thought to be in Manchester as well as London if, while I am at the London meeting, I am able also to cause someone to stumble and fall under a bus in Manchester, or cause a knife or other missile to pierce his body. If I had such a power and exercised it in this way, it would obviously be very difficult to trace the action to me. It would presumably have to be established that I was possessed of the extraordinary power involved, and if I always kept secret about it, it would be hard to associate with me. I might be thought to be a person with a strong motive, but that could hardly begin to count on its own in a case of this kind. If I myself, for some reason, made my intention known this would help, but in the absence of a substantial number of similar cases, it would not be taken very seriously, and if it were taken seriously it might, nonetheless, be a case of precognition. A pattern of paranormal power on my part would have to be established and the act would have to carry some particular style or other characteristic attributable to me. But even with this, a motive and even a statement of intention, we would still be in the realm of very vague conjecture until the day arrives, if it ever will, when the exercise of paranormal powers, as we now think of them, admits of precise determination. The most that I could be seriously accused of in practice would be terrifying the credulous or making myself in some like way a nuisance – or, if some offensive ritual were involved, blasphemy perhaps.

It is known of course that, from time to time, certain poor wretches have been subjected to the cruellest treatment on suspicion of practising some form of witchcraft. But this only attests to the credulity, superstitious bias, and unreasoning hatred to which people are liable at times. There is no proper test that could be applied, and if any legal action were taken it would be on the grounds of exercising improper psychological influence or causing distress to the simple-minded. In any case, causation at a distance is only a very weak form of being in two places at once. It would not normally set us asking questions about a divided personality. The initiative for all that happens would be thought to come from the same source. The case in which we might be seriously concerned as to whether we should think of two persons rather than one would be that in which two bodies are involved. Is it then conceivable that one person should have more than one physical body at the same time?

The claim that this is, in fact, not only conceivable, but does happen has indeed been extensively made. In Eastern countries it is not thought to be nearly as preposterous as it would seem to us in the West. A holy man can be sitting, deep in meditation, in the calm of his Himalayan retreat and, at the same time, be wandering through the villages teaching or helping the needy or engaged on some other mission far away. Some can materialise, so it is alleged, with very little warning or preparation wherever their presence is needed. The new second body does not always resemble the normal one, and it is thus possible to materialise as required incognito. Are these, then, possibilities we can consider seriously?

We must not be too daunted here by the almost total absence of evidence – or, at least, of evidence that can be

effectively checked. For many things may happen which
can not in fact be confirmed. But it is worth asking, though
this is not the major issue, how the claim that one has been
in two places at once could be established. Presumably, as
in the case of alleged pre-existence, much would turn on
one's being able to describe what went on in both places
without being told or learning in some normal way. This
could be clairvoyance, but, if there were no ascertainable
continuous history of the alleged second embodiment, as
evidenced by others, or, more positively, if it could be
shown that it had disappeared without trace, then the
hypothesis of a new 'materialisation' would be much streng-
thened, whatever we thought of the strictly physical properties of the second body – others would have seen and
presumably touched it. But what matters at the moment is
not the testability of these claims, in point of fact, but their
inherent possibility.

To consider this further we must again draw a distinction
between a weak and a strong form of the possibility considered. In the weak form all we need suppose is that some
person is able to cause a bodily form, a wraith or appearance, to present itself to certain observers and go through
the motions normally attributed to purposive action. There
would be no real duplication of full embodiment. It would
be more a case of creating an illusion of immediate
bodily presence and not very far removed from
straightforward causation at a distance. In the strong
form there would be full double embodiment. A person
would be as much involved with the second body as with
the first, he would have two properly physical bodies and
function alike and continuously in both. The supposition
that this is possible is a peculiarly difficult one to entertain. On any reasonable account we are very much
involved with our bodies. The dualist should not question
this, and I shall return to the point again. We have a
'body image', of which more in a moment. We perceive
things in the external world from a 'point of view' determined by the location of our bodies. We have so-called
'physical' sensations located, in some sense, in the body.
There is constant interaction of the mind and the brain.

Would all this be possible, in a full-blooded sense with two bodies – or more?

It will be plain that this is not a situation like our minding or managing two machines, or riding one horse and leading the other. We do not 'manage' our bodies in that way; we function through them in a much completer fashion. A point of view and the various functions of the brain and nervous system give us a co-ordinated experience without which life as we know it would hardly be possible. Could this be repeated for a single mind without confusion and a conflation of experiences which would at once become chaotic? If that is to be avoided it must be possible for the one mind to be constantly viewing two different scenes in a continuous and co-ordinated way, to hold together two very different sets of thinking and purposing at a fully conscious level, in short to live two fully rounded lives at the same time. That would be a most astonishing feat, and the onus thus lies on those who maintain, with little serious thought as a rule, that a person can, in the strong sense, be in two places at once and an occupant of two bodies such that two persons, as they seem to the outsider, could both have the genuine, and not merely pseudo, memories of a person who lived in the past – the onus lies on the one who maintains this to come effectively to terms with the quite extraordinary character of the claim he is making. At first glance the odds are all against it.

And yet we should not be too hasty. I have indicated the obvious difficulties. But we need to remember also how varied and complicated are our accomplishments and experiences at any particular time as things are. At the moment I am pursuing my present train of thought, but I am also directing the pen across the paper. My other fingers hold the paper in its place. I perceive the table and some books and papers on it. Lifting my head a little I see and admire the Jersey cows in the field. I am aware of physical sensations of various kinds and much else in 'the margin' of attention. All this is, in fact, made possible, as we now know, by the proper functioning of the brain and nervous system. Without that there could not be the necessary co-ordination under the normal conditions of our lives.

But we are not normally conscious of these conditions. I do not issue instructions to my brain or manipulate it in any way. I just decide to write and do so. There is therefore no inherent difficulty on the mental side in managing several things at once. The question then remains whether this may not in principle admit of vast extension; and, with drastic alteration of the causal conditions, what might the limit be? We should not be too hasty to legislate from what we find normally, or even invariably, the case at present to what is in principle possible.

Perhaps we approximate to the situation of managing two, or more, lives, as it were, in reverie or the curious condition of being half-awake and half in a dream. I am walking through the fields, mounting the stiles and generally getting along without stumbling, enjoying the sun and the smell of new-mown hay; but I am also 'miles away', holding conversation perhaps with a group of philosophers in London – or enjoying yet warmer sun in Miami. I visualise the beach at Key Biscayne and seem to myself to be strolling around there. Admittedly I am not, in fact, in Miami. No one would know where my thoughts were if I did not tell him. Nothing is changed in Miami, the real holiday-makers there do not see me, there is no imprint in the sands. I am still causally conditioned by my one brain and body. But mentally I approximate to being in two places; and, if the present causal conditions were suspended or modified, it would be conceivable that I should, in the course of my reverie, have some actual clairvoyant vision of what is going on, on the distant beach, and by telekinesis be able also to effect some change there. This still falls short of being in the fullest sense in Miami and at home. But it would set us on the way to having a double life, and there might thus be such an extension as would really involve having proper perceptual awareness of the beach from a point of view on another body, physical and somatic sensations there as well as here and two main trains of thought. This would indeed be a very considerable extension, and the variation in the causal conditions involved in having two brains, etc. would be exceptionally drastic – too drastic perhaps for us to envisage effectively. Can we entertain the possibility? The most

that I will say here is that we should not be too hasty in dismissing it.

One point needs, however, to be much stressed. It is that,
if we are to think seriously of two persons, as they seem to
us or outwardly, being in fact one person, we must insist on
there being awareness in one life of what goes on in the
other in the same way as there is in itself. I must, in both
cases, be aware of my experiences in having them. Otherwise, we would only have some very weak sense of 'two persons' being also one. In terms of the account of persons and
their identity given above, a person is aware of his experience, and of himself as the one unique being who has it, in
the process of having any experience. This is compatible
with our forgetting many experiences we have had and, in
this way, of a great deal of one's life being occluded from
the rest – very sharply in serious loss of memory or so-called
'split-personality'. For here we become unaware of something that is now over. But at the time of having an experience we cannot fail to be aware of having it, however little
we attend to it or reflect upon it. When the experiences are
simultaneous in the purported seeming two lives, the one
being who has them must, on my view, be equally aware of
both. How much he retains of one or the other in conscious
thought immediately after, or in memory dispositionally, is
another matter. Perhaps the business of leading two 'lives'
could be eased by some mechanism of rapidly switching
attention or swiftly dismissing the events of the one from
one's thoughts to mind the other. But we could not do too
much of this if the events of one life are not to become
wholly chaotic. If the two lives are normal lives, we need
to be minding both. That is what we must envisage, two
perceptual points of view, two different sets of purposing,
etc., if we are to think seriously of one person being for
any length of time fully in two places; and it seems that we
must think of it as a continuous condition if we are to
think of two seemingly different persons having the genuine, and not the pseudo, memories of Guy Fawkes, and
thus being, in fact, one person. This would be the case,
likewise, if the memories were repeated or afterwards
themselves remembered, for they would be occurring in

the one consciousness which has the purported double embodiment.

The difficulties which these suppositions present on any view which takes them seriously and not in the very limited senses required in the artistic license of fiction, highlight for us the difficulty of our envisaging any kind of existence which is not subject to severe limitations as a condition of its being a meaningful co-ordinated experience. This, in turn, strongly suggests some kind of embodiment or its equivalent. I do not think that embodiment is the way we become particularised, as is often held in doctrines of 'a universal mind' – far from it, indeed, if my main contentions are sound. But any conceivable finite existence seems to require inevitably some limiting medium through which it is sustained and by which it expresses itself. What infinite existence, or transcendent being, must be like is entirely beyond our comprehension. But there must be some limiting medium for finite being and thus, if not a physical body, its analogue or some other means of focusing and limiting experience.

This will concern us again. But, in the meantime, the present considerations lead us naturally to the point where we must note more closely than has hitherto been possible the peculiarly close involvement of all of us, in our existence as we now know it, in our bodies. The dualist, as was stressed, ignores this at his peril, and I must, therefore, adjust the balance of our discussion in this regard before we go further.

7 The Importance of the Body

Account has already been taken of a person's peculiarly close involvement with his body in the conditions to which we are normally subject in our present existence. The dualist, as was also stressed, has no need to deny this, and it is very unwise for him to do so. One obvious form of this involvement, and the one with which we have been mainly concerned hitherto, is the causal one. Our mental states are conditioned by physical ones. This is a simple matter of experience for all. If I fall asleep I have only dream thoughts. If I am tired my thoughts are sluggish, or if in a fever my thoughts are delirious. Hit me on the head and I may have no thoughts or sensations at all, or cut my finger with a knife and I am in pain. I say that this is simple in the sense that the most simple-minded person is aware of it, even brutes. At a more sophisticated level we understand better how this comes about. We know about the nervous system and the circulation of the blood and the special function of the brain; and experts are learning about this today in ways that go far beyond the grasp of the layman. No one seriously doubts the closeness of our involvement with the body in this sense.

It does not follow, as has also been stressed, that the states of our bodies determine exhaustively the states of our minds. They condition them, but that is a very different thing. The main determinant of the course of one's thoughts is the nature of those thoughts themselves. If this were not the case almost all that we do would be pointless. This has already been sufficiently stressed, and I leave the matter there.

But the body is involved in other ways, and more intimately, in the kind of experience we have. It helps more directly in making possible the awareness we have of the world around us. For the location and posture of the body determine our perceptual experience. Various accounts may be given of perception. But, on any view, we must reckon with the infinite gradation of changes according to the location of one's body and related conditions, 'perspectival distortion' as it is technically called. This is a very remarkable phenomenon, and it has set philosophers pondering and arguing about the nature or status of the world disclosed in perception from very early times. Some philosophers of today have tried to by-pass the problems so engendered by appeals to ordinary language or the paradigm use of words. It certainly strikes us all as odd to suppose that I am looking at flying patches of sense data when I watch a race, or that I lean my elbow now on a patch of colour in my visual field – 'we are looking at horses', it will be said, and my elbow is 'resting on the table'. But this may show no more than how difficult it is to find a satisfactory way of handling the problems of perception and talking about them. However averse we may be to speculation, we just cannot deny that the world which we normally take for granted is a very odd one on any account. My perceptions do, in fact, change from moment to moment, whatever the philosophical account to be given of this. Objects do look small in the distance, mis-shapen when observed through a faulty glass pane, square when we know them to be round, red when we view them through red-coloured glasses. The problems presented by this are a subject in themselves, and in spite of all that Plato said about 'the long and circuitous route' that philosophers must take, we must set ourselves a limit. Suffice it then for us to note these perspectival changes and the most remarkable way in which they dove-tail into one another with invariable co-ordination of change and circumstance. To anyone who reflects, this is one of the most truly astonishing and impressive features of our experience, and it should clearly have more prominence than is usually given it by those who invoke 'the argument from design' in discussions of the existence of God.

In the absence of the kind of co-ordination noted, experience would be too chaotic for us to survive except, if at all, in a very rudimentary form of transitory life of mere sensation. Even in dreams there is much co-ordination, and dreams are usually, perhaps always, parasitic on waking experience. If perceptions occurred in a random way, the wildest world of dreams would take over. But one of the central ways of averting that disaster is that our perceptual experience is co-ordinated from a 'point of view' determined by the location and position of our bodies. Details of the mechanism by which this is accomplished do not concern us now. The brain has obviously a great deal to do with it. But the fact remains that the way we actually perceive things in visual experience, and in co-ordination with that in other modes of perception, is made possible by remarkable correlations of all our perceptions with the location of the body and the discriminatory functioning, if we may so call it, of our sense organs. The suggestion has been made from time to time (for example, in the kind of Naive Realism sponsored at one period by Bertrand Russell) that what our sense organs do is to blot out an almost infinite number of surfaces we might see or touch, etc., or to block a vast number of sensations we might otherwise have. Not many hold this view now and there may be little substance in it. But the thought of it will give some indication of the highly selective function of sense perception, whatever the final account of it. At present, at least, all this is made possible for us by our having the kinds of bodies we do have.

Would it then be possible if we had a different kind of body, different that is in some essential way and not just as the bodies of various terrestrial creatures differ, or if we had no bodies at all? It is hard for us to envisage a wholly disembodied state, but if there were such a state it would still be necessary to have some way of limiting and focusing the kind of experiences we did have. There would also be a peculiarly difficult problem about communication. But these are questions to which we shall be returning shortly.

It is through our bodies also that we make ourselves effective in the world around us. There is nothing inconceivable in the idea of causation at a distance. I can imagine myself lifting my arm, and books at the far end of the table rising in the air at my gesture, or just in response to my wish. It is a mystery to us, I have maintained, that we can control our bodies, a mystery that remains when we have noted all we know about the brain and its relation to the rest of one's body. The structure of the brain is undoubtedly essential for the co-ordination of our movements as we find things. But, as has been much stressed, this does not account for the initial impact of thought on matter, and we can at least conceive things being very different. Indeed, we make great play with such possibilities in various kinds of fiction and in any kindred talk about magic. The fairy waves her wand and is at once transported elsewhere, or a turnip at her wish becomes a carriage. The witch rides her broom and causes the milk to turn sour. Whether there are claims to such powers which deserve serious examination, other than the paranormal influence of minds on minds in the first instance, and how they should be assessed, are difficult questions which we need not consider now. The question of miracles would be involved as well. It would certainly be an advantage on many occasions if, by magic or in some religious way, we could change things other than through our bodies. We might effect cures of grave illnesses or help ourselves or others in distress. Who would hesitate to use such powers or not feel the moral duty to do so in some circumstances? If I could avert a flood by magically throwing a dam across the river, or if I could throw a magic rope to a man trapped in a burning room, it seems plain that I ought to do so. But most of us, most of the time at least, are confined to what we can do through our bodies.

It is also important that this, or at least its equivalent, should be the case. However trying we may find our limitations to be, when a little extension to our reach perhaps could save a life, our lives would at once become impossible if we all had unlimited magical power. Indeed, even magic is only conceivable within certain limitations; there has to be some kind of stability to give anything any character or nature at all. If we all began to change things at will there would be chaos. Nothing could be contrived against the future nor, without exceptional understanding and trust, could there be any combining with others in joint undertakings. We can indeed envisage a world in which the conditions were different in some important respects, and I shall refer to attempts to do this in a moment. But there must clearly be some rigid conditions and limitations if we are to have an environment in which we can function. At present the limit is set by what we can do through our bodies in the world around us; and this gives us all a very fundamental way in which we feel at one with our bodies. It is in our bodies that we move and have our being in the world; and it is not surprising for this reason that we should come to think and speak of our bodies a good deal of the time as just ourselves. They are ourselves in operation; and while we sometimes extend this to motor-cars or other devices and say such things as 'I was going at sixty miles an hour' or 'I capsized', the use we make of a car or a boat is still intermittent and restricted. Our bodies are involved in endless varieties of ways all the time and much more directly than any machine. It is understandable that some should be led in this way, though very mistakenly, to identify themselves literally with their bodies. The body, as our sole way of being effective in the world, is obviously of prime importance. We cherish it for this as for other reasons.

The involvement becomes even closer through the way our so-called 'physical sensations' have, in some fundamental sense, their seat or location in the body. We are sensitive in our bodies. I touch things with my fingers, and while more is involved in the touching than having sensations, the sensation itself is in my fingers, as we normally think of it. If someone touches me, or if I run into the corner of the table, I feel myself being touched in a particular spot. I locate these sensations at once and without difficulty. If my eyes are shut I know all the same that I am being touched on the back of my hand and not on the nape of my neck. I can also feel pain in some special part of my body, and indeed this is the form pain normally takes, though it has sometimes a rather vague diffusion and at times we 'ache all over'. I do not have to wonder whether the pain is in my foot or in my finger, in my forehead or in my tooth. Nor do I have to see the swelling or the cut on my foot to know that I am in pain. I could have both the former, under local anaesthetic, without any actual pain. The cause of the pain may also be other than I take it. All have heard nowadays of 'referred' pains. But whatever the doctor may say about where the trouble is, I am the one who can tell him in the first place where it hurts. As a rule I have no doubt. I feel the pain 'in my chest' or 'in my finger'.

This raises some peculiarly difficult questions, most of all, at first glance at least, for the dualist. How do we know that the pain is in the finger and not in the foot? In practice there is not, as a rule, any problem – 'I just feel it there', we say. If pressed, the layman is apt to talk of nerves and tissue and something being 'relayed' to the brain. But this physiological story, however sound, does not help here. I do not need to know anything of it, any more than of the swelling, to know that it is my finger that hurts. The causal explanation does not explain how I, who may or may not know of these physiological factors, know at once where it hurts. The dog knows just as well or the cow when it rubs its itching back against the post. There seems to be some immediate locating of sensations.

But we also place touches, tickles, aches and pains, etc. on the mental side of our dichotomy. No one can strictly observe my pain, as I was stressing earlier. You can observe the cause of it, or hear my account of it, but the pain itself is private, it is what I feel; I undergo, suffer or experience it. There can be no pain that is not felt, but feeling the pain is a mental process. Hence, the dilemma. We have some mental reality which is also located and thus extended in space. This is a further argument, and a very strong one, used by those who object to a wedge being sharply driven, as I have been doing, between mind and body; and this is the context where it becomes very plausible to suggest that we would do better to talk of 'embodied minds'.

A person who has taken just this course is Professor G.N.A. Vesey. He does this in a short but incisive book entitled *The Embodied Mind*. There seem to be two main themes to this book. The first of these involves the teaching of James Ward about the essential inter-dependence of subject and object in all experience. We noted this above and I readily conceded that, on the subject side, we could not think of a mere subject of experience without any content experienced. The self must be or do something; it could not exist in a void, notwithstanding that its existence is not bound up with having any particular experience. But Ward was also emphatic that the self must be actual, and we must add that, even on a Berkeleyan or phenomenalist view of the external world, we cannot regard the content presented to us in perception as being exhausted in the fact of being perceived. This is not only because of the co-ordinated character of our perceptions, but also because, in the case of vision at least, there is some character of being 'over-against-us' in our sense presentations. The table, as perceived, is not, on any plausible view, just a modification of my mind. What status we accord to the external world is a further question, and opinions will differ about it. My point at the moment is that we cannot, on the basis of some kind of polarity of subject and object in experience, avoid asking the questions to which dualism seems to me the proper answer. To talk of 'the embodied mind' does not, in respect of the present issue, advance the subject at all.

Vesey's other main concern is with the location of sensations like tickles and pains, and he argues for the view that, in these cases as also in the case of sounds, we locate the pain or the sound directly. Even if I do not locate a sound with precision, I hear it 'coming from the left and not from the right', etc. The last point does not seem to me to be Vesey's strongest suit. Hearing sounds is a complicated matter, quite apart from the complicated mechanism by which it happens. We may at one moment be certain that we actually hear the gunfire from our left but, after being told that the range is straight ahead, hear it coming from there. Even close at hand we may 'swear' that the scrabbling of mice behind the wainscot is just behind our backs and have a quite different impression when we learn that it is a case of birds who could only get in on the other side. Our impression may change merely by being told this, not because the mice run around – or, in the first example, because the wind shifts. This should predispose us to caution also in the case of pain. But it must be admitted that, in most cases of pain or touch, we seem to know immediately 'where it is'. If I shut my eyes and put both hands on the table for someone to touch the back of one hand, then I know at once which hand it is. I feel the touch in the place that I would see if I looked.

The traditional answer to this problem is along the lines of what is usually called 'the local sign' theory. In essentials this holds that we come to associate certain sensations with parts of the body which we learn in the course of experience to be connected with them. This is usually some part of the body which I can withdraw, for example, to avoid unpleasant sensations, or advance to have agreeable ones. This would be more plausible if there were a very sharp difference of quality corresponding to the different parts of the body on which our sensations are located. But while there are such differences between a pain and a touch, or between being pricked by the point of a pencil and being gently carressed, there seems to be no obvious difference between being pricked by a pencil on one hand and on the other. A pain in my toe can be very like a pain in my finger. Pains do seem to differ in quality, a toothache and a stomach ache for instance, though how much this is really a difference in quality and not just in intensity and association, is not so certain. But the point is that the differences do not seem to be marked in all cases where we locate a pain without hesitating, as in pricks on the back of one hand and on the other – or on a leg.

To meet this, the advocates of the local sign theory, or some successor to it by other names, maintain that the essential associations were set up in very early infancy when we were learning about our bodies the things we subsequently come to know as a matter of course – very young children it appears have great difficulty in locating pains. A baby does not know its body as we do; he has to 'discover it'. Subtle associations are set up in these ways which later become automatic and unreflective. An excellent statement of this argument is found in C.A. Campbell's *On Selfhood and Godhood*. Vesey refers closely to it and rests his main objection on the lack of a sufficiently distinctive quale for the sensations involved as they now come into mature experience.

My own view is that some solution must be found along the lines indicated by Campbell, but I also feel that this is a case where a great deal more work needs to be done by philosophers, working in close collaboration with psychologists, to probe further into the way we locate things and the part which formative experience will have played in this; and it may be that, when such study is further advanced, the aspect of it which is most baffling now may not be so difficult to accord with what, on all other counts, we seem forced to believe.

It would certainly seem strained to make the main weight of the case for some doctrine of embodied mind, as an alternative to dualism, rest on the difficulties connected with the way we locate physical sensations; for however uncertain we may be about our approach to this problem and its implications, the fact remains that we find experience by its very nature to be the kind of reality which cannot as such have spatial extension, however much it may apprise us of extended things. The problems of our 'physical' sensations are thus a challenge to further investigation rather than to the essentials of a dualist view.

At the same time the involvement with the body is peculiarly close in regard to the physical sensations just noted. This applies also to 'somatic sensations', which we feel continuously but more vaguely within rather than on the surface of the body. The part played by what psychologists call the body-image, the body in its felt totality to oneself in distinction from what we learn otherwise about it, is prominent also in creating the impression of our almost being the body itself in some respects.

The place of the body in communication was noted earlier. This calls for further comment. There can be no doubt that it is through our bodies that we normally communicate with one another. The precise account of the way this happens is a further matter, and opinions about it will differ sharply. But it seems plain that the way I normally learn what a person is like and what he thinks is by seeing or hearing him or reading what he writes or listening to him on the radio and television or some kindred device. I need not see or hear him myself. Indeed we have very important communications addressed expressly to ourselves, like a note from the Tax Inspector, from persons we have never seen or met in a strict sense. We learn much about persons who have been dead a long time when we read their writings or learn about them in a host of other ways; if we come across the cave or hut in which some Robinson Crusoe lived we may learn a great deal about the way he fended for himself, although he himself took no steps to make this known. In most cases where we learn about people we have not met ourselves, it is known that other people have done so. At some point in the line which brings me my note from the Tax Inspector, there will be people who have seen or heard him, and it is on the presumption that this is the case that I take him seriously. In the case of those who have not put anything in writing of some kind, as in the notable instances of Socrates and Jesus[1], there were still many who did see and hear them if we are to place any credence on the subsequent records. Whether distorted or not, the evidence must have been first-hand in the first place. This is what we normally presuppose, and whether we are thinking of people in remote times or today, the usual way in which we know what they are like is from evidence of those who have seen or heard them – or by doing so ourselves.

There could be cases, as in examples noted earlier, of some communication from creatures whom no one in this world has seen, 'people' from outer space, for instance, whose messages come to us solely in signs or signals for which we discover the code. We assume that such beings are seen or heard by one another, and that they are not wholly unlike ourselves. Even if they were not in fact seen or heard or otherwise directly observed by one another, but only communicated in the signals they transmitted, we assume again that they have bodies of some kind by which they produce the signals which others read. If not, we are close to the border – if not beyond it – for anything which could come within the terms 'normal communication'. But even here we do depend on marks, detectable in some way, in the observable world. The communication comes through physical media.

It would be possible, I suppose, to imagine some denizen of this world, a human being like ourselves, who had been kept in isolation from birth, and thus never directly observed, but cared for and instructed and educated sufficiently to make his wishes known and perhaps even have fairly full contacts in some respects with the world outside. He learns what buttons and switches to press and so forth. But this again requires physical media which are controlled at some stage by a person's body. The simplest and commonest case of learning about one another and communicating is where we directly perceive one another's bodies. This seems to be the standard case.

Moreover, even when we think of paranormal ways of communicating, like telepathy, the presumption is that the persons concerned have been known and identified in the first instance in normal ways – they will have been seen and heard, etc. Telepathy is rare, and the confirmation we seek for it is in terms of what can be established otherwise. I receive a message from Brown that he is in distress in Paris, and I learn afterwards from asking him and others that this was, in fact, the case. One might, of course, have telepathic messages, if we allow them, from someone we do not know and whom others are unable to trace. But how would I know that these messages, using the term broadly for any information emanating from him, do really come from this, or indeed from any outside source. Presumably we would pay much heed to the distinctness and soundness of the 'information'. If I seemed to have messages every time a race was run tipping me the winner, or information about take-over bids on the Stock Exchange, and these proved invariably correct, I would certainly take this to be more than accident, and might wish to take some advantage of it. But I, or someone on my behalf, would be checking the seeming information by observations involving our senses. Nor would we be likely to entertain the idea of telepathy in a case of this sort unless we had acquired some confidence in it, as a likely occurrence, from cases in which the communication came from sources which we were able to identify in the normal way initially. To establish it otherwise, and to know that the communications came, on every occasion, from the same source, would be very difficult. And what would it be like to 'seem to have a message'? I leave this for the moment, merely making the point that telepathy, and other paranormal communications, such as messages from the dead, normally occur in a context where those concerned can be, or have in the past been, identified through their bodies.

Let us keep, for the present then, to normal communication. Here the body is obviously involved. The simplest case seems to be that in which a person is, as we put it, visibly or bodily present. My friend calls and I learn that he is very sad. How do I learn this? Because he looks sad or he tells me of his grief. But what I strictly see or hear is his face and the posture of his body, in the one case, the sounds he utters in the other. This has sometimes been queried. It is said, for example, that I do not just see the drawn or contorted face, or drooping shoulders. These adjectives themselves imply more than a physical object or presentation. We see someone looking sad and we hear speech. So it is argued. But this argument does not seem to me sound. The sadness is not a quality or disposition of the face, nor are the sounds strictly sad. The sadness is a way a person feels or thinks, it is a strictly mental state. We do, of course speak of a 'plaintive' note or a sad or dull look, but this may be metaphor or the convenient mode of speech for rough and ready purposes. There is no strict perception of sadness. What is visible is the colour of skin, the shape and movement of bodily features. But I have no difficulty in immediately recognising my friend and understanding what he feels and thinks. This is normally so straightforward that we make no note of the immediate movement of our own thought from what is presented to what we believe to be a person's state of mind. Knowledge of other persons is not strictly direct, least of all in normal circumstances. It is mediated. Only the other person himself knows immediately what he thinks or feels. We learn about it, usually at least, through states of the body. A state of mind can not as such be observed.

This is implied in most that has been argued hitherto. But we must now note two objections that relate especially to the present state of our discussion. The first of these is that mediated awareness of other persons seems to deprive our relationships of the warmth and spontaneity which is so important for them. A philosopher of considerable note and influence, namely Cook Wilson, put this in striking and oft-quoted terms when he remarked that he did not want just 'inferred friends'[2]. He wanted real or close ones, and it must be admitted that the idea of an inference from someone's appearance or words to what lies 'beyond' them can seem artificial or inhibiting. But the point of this is that 'inference' may not perhaps be the best word; it conveys too strong an impression of a calculated deliberate movement of thought. To that extent 'mediation' is perhaps a better term. But we must not obscure the fact that our thought moves, in learning about other people, from what is just physically presented to an understanding of what is not at all extended or physical, namely a state of mind. The body gives us our clue. We learn to read it, and, as has already been stressed, we normally do this so easily and dependably that there is no serious sense of inhibition or restraint. We just meet and talk.

A position that is closely related to that of Cook Wilson, and which owes not a little to him in recent presentations of it, is that of Martin Buber and his followers. They seem to hold that we can have some intimation of another's mind which is not properly knowlege about it. I have elsewhere[3] considered in some detail the now famous distinction between '*I – Thou*' and '*I – It*', and I have indicated what seem to me most important insights of Martin Buber as well as some abuses of these and misunderstandings of what they meant. Here it must suffice to say that it is hard to see what the alleged 'relation' of mind to mind can be that is not rooted in what we learn or think about one another. We react to one another on the basis of what we take other people's thoughts and attitudes to be like. Without this there can be no substance in our relationships or dealings with each other. The bearing of this consideration on other questions, and especially the question of any ultimate destiny we may have in fellowship with God, will be noted later. Suffice it for the moment to observe that we find no way to by-pass the problem of our knowledge of one another in the suggestion that we have some immediate characterless relation with one another, even if this is thought to supervene upon 'knowledge about'. All that matters in our relationships, most of all the most rich and intimate ones, depends directly on what we think and feel about one another, and what we intend, and all this, in turn, depends on mediation through non-mental physical means. This is also a matter much overlooked in accounts of so-called 'disclosure situations' by which some followers of Buber today seek to get by without raising the usual problems about 'other minds'.

Some consequences of the mediated character of our knowledge of one another will be noted later. But let us now proceed to the second of the objections of which I wish to take account here. This concerns the manner of the alleged mediation. What, it may be asked, is the justification of the alleged movement of our thought from the bodily states that we observe (looks, sounds, movements, etc.) to the corresponding state of mind? A possible answer would be that we establish the appropriate correlations in the same way as we normally learn about the world around us, that is by observing regularities and concomitant variations. But this will not quite do in the present case. For, *ex hypothesi*, we do not observe the mental states. We might argue that, when a person screams or wrings his finger or clasps his head, he is in pain, for this is the sort of thing that people do when they are in pain. But then how do we know in the first instance that someone who screams or wrings his finger is in pain at the time? He will tell us, we may be told. But this only throws it all a stage further back. How do we know that the sounds he utters convey to us what he feels or thinks? There seems to be no way of getting on to the 'inner' or properly mental side of the process to establish our correlations in the first place. Minds are occluded from immediate view, or, more strictly, they can not be viewed at all.

This has been taken by many today to be virtually axiomatic in the refutation of dualism and any supposed movement of thought from physical clues to mental states. The prominence given to the objection by Ryle was noted earlier. It is in this connection that he offers us his well-known analogy of the signal box. We establish connections between the positions and movements of the signals or the rails and the pulling of levers in the signal box because we can inspect both. Anyone can walk into the signal box, but we cannot enter people's minds in the same way. The force of this argument has been a major factor in inclining many philosophers today towards some form of behaviourist or identity thesis. Even those who otherwise favour a dualist position feel so daunted by the present difficulty that they hold back, as in A. J. Ayer's retreat to what he calls 'a middle way', depending upon the insistence that the body is at least indispensable to establish continued identity. But even if we were to allow the last claim, in one's own case as in that of others, and thereby make the body more essential to the notion of our own identity, it would still provide little easement directly to the present problem. If, on the other hand, we deny outright that mental processes are distinct from physical ones, if the smile I observe *is* my friend's happiness, if the sounds he utters are themselves the greetings he brings me, we are certainly rid of our present quandary, but at what a price! The price is the surrender of all that seems most evident in what we understand about our mental states and processes.

If we are not to pay this price what recourse have we? In the past it was thought that a solution could be found by stressing the analogy, or close resemblance, between one's own body and that of others. I know at least what my own states of mind are – the thesis begins with this assumption; and I note the states of my own body when I also find myself in certain mental states. I hold my head when I have a head-ache, and when others do this they are likewise presumably in pain. But the bodily responses of various people, or of oneself at different times, do not follow quite so rigid a pattern as this seems to require. A headache does not always lead me to clasp my brow, and when people do this they do it in different ways and sometimes when they have no pain at all, but are sunk in deep thought. Nor do we usually take very close note of the disposition of our own bodies. Furthermore, we communicate extensively with people who are not bodily present to us, on radio, television, in writing and so on; and I have noted already the possibility of communicating confidently with people about whose bodies we may have no information, creatures in outer space, for example.

It seems, therefore, that we must not rely on analogy in the strict sense. But we have something very similar which was, I suspect, the serious intention of those who used the unfortunate term 'analogy'. We do not just observe our own bodily movements and note that in point of fact they take a certain course when we are in certain states of mind; we intend them, and we do so, not in some random way but as the appropriate means of achieving certain ends. I reach for the cake because this is how I can eat it, I draw my hands away from the hot plate to avoid burning. I clasp my hand to where my brow aches because this eases the pain or helps me to endure it. When I see other bodies behaving in a similar way, I conclude, obviously with justification, that the movement is intended in that case also to serve some purpose which it seems readily to meet. An isolated movement of this sort might not take us very far, but when we observe an endless variation of movements, patterned to serve what appear to be appropriate purposes and subtly varied to meet variations and changes in the circumstances, and when there seems to be no other reason why these bodies should behave as they do, then surely the proper conclusion to draw is that they are animated and directed by minds functioning substantially as we do ourselves.[4]

The position here is not unlike the argument from design in religious thought. We seem to be living in an ordered or patterned world. Life would indeed not be possible otherwise. We plan and anticipate what will happen, and within this we find the marvellously intelligible intricacies of perspectival adjustment and the physical organs which sustain it, all this responsive in turn to the infinite intelligible variations in the world of nature at large which the scientist discloses to us in all its remarkable detail. By these means there is, moreover, sustained an existence that is rich in worth-while attainment and sensitive response; and, accordingly, some suppose that there must be some master mind or supreme designer who keeps 'the stars in their courses' and maintains all the dependable microscopic detail of the world as we find it. Whether this argument holds when we think of the world as a whole, and how within the terms of it we might cope with the disturbing realities of suffering and other evils, are questions we cannot embark upon now; and it must be stressed that the effectiveness of the argument in the case of God does not affect its soundness as applied generally to other minds. But it is surely a natural movement of thought, if we find some pattern of events which we could not expect to come about in the normal course of things, to seek an explanation in terms of some intelligent purposive agency. The infinitely varied co-ordinated movements of what we describe as animate bodies, and most of all the bodies of other persons, as we inevitably think of them, are of this sort. The obvious explanation is a sensitive agent, and this, I submit, is what we all normally take for granted.

We have therefore no need to be perturbed because we are unable to inspect or look in on one another's thoughts and feelings directly. It is indeed hard to conceive what this would be like. Nor is it clear that we would desire it. Some thoughts we certainly prefer to keep to ourselves. All the same we have all the reason we need for ascribing certain thoughts and other experiences to other persons as the obvious explanation of the state and behaviour of their bodies. We know what it is to have various experiences ourselves, and the state and movements of various bodies we observe become easily intelligible to us if we consider them to be animated by beings who have similar experiences. This seems the obvious explanation, and in the absence of it we would be quite bewildered by these particular changes and states. There is not usually a conscious effort of interpretation, or any noticeable time lag. It all happens smoothly and easily, though there are some occasions when we are perplexed; and this is why it seems odd at first to say that we make inferences about other people's states of mind rather than just say that we hear, understand, see them. But the fact remains that all we directly perceive is a bodily state which at once indicates to us a state of mind. We manage this normally without a conscious effort and in an easy and most expeditious way. Nor is there normally any reason to doubt the soundness and reliability of this procedure.

This does not mean that there is no possibility at all of error. In theory we could be mistaken, not just in this or that instance, but generally. That is, we might be wrong in supposing that the bodies which seem to be animate are, in fact, so. This is what so many find disturbing. A. J. Ayer, for example, expresses his concern that if the ascription of consciousness to other things is based on 'inference from their behaviour, it is at least possible that I am the only person in the world'[5]. He seems to think we should never entertain this possibility. But provisionally we must do so to understand better what precisely is wrong with it. It will not do simply to declare that we all in fact believe it to be mistaken. We must ask 'Why?' and to do this we must recognise a theoretical possibility that what we take to be the bodies of persons just happen by some odd turn of things to behave consistently as if they were animate or, more plausibly, that some superior creature, like Descartes's demon, has ingeniously contrived and manipulated it all to appear animate when, in fact, it is not so. This is a theoretical possibility, but we have no reason to suppose that we are being deceived by such a demon and, as we have an obvious explanation in terms of conscious and purposed behaviour, we can readily dismiss the theoretical possibility and grant it only the remotest degree of possibility which need not disturb us in any measure.

It does not follow that we may not often be mistaken in particular cases. We do, in fact, sometimes misunderstand, and it may be that we never completely understand one another. Much of our human situation turns on this, and composers of fiction have often exploited it. But while there may be occasional or partial misunderstanding we remain reasonably confident that we have a fair understanding of one another's thoughts and feelings. If we could place no confidence in what we seem to learn about one another, by express communication or indirectly, life would be impossible. In some cases our confidence is stronger, depending upon the level at which it is claimed and the extent of our acquaintance with various people. A matter of fact request, for the time of the next train to London, for example, or for the salt at table, is not easily misunderstood. There are other thoughts which are 'too deep for words'. The wider context in which something is disclosed may also make a difference to its full import. It may be very hard to grasp anything in its fullness in personal relationships. Some people are more perceptive and understanding than others, and some, like ministers or doctors or psychiatrists, acquire special skills for the purpose. But that is not our problem now. Granting that our knowledge and understanding of one another is incomplete and variable, we nonetheless take it for granted that we do know one another well in some respects and deal with each other on this basis. We trust what we learn on the basis of observed behaviour, taking the term in its widest sense.

On this general question we have no serious doubt, whatever the degree of uncertainty we have in particular cases. There remains a remote theoretical doubt, and if we are so troubled by this that we wish to remove it altogether, as Ayer seems to do in the passage quoted, then the price is a high one. It involves the surrender of what we consider most distinctive of mental states, their *sui generis* character, and this is not, I believe, a surrender which Ayer is prepared to make. If we can somehow identify the mental state with its manifestation, the joy with the smile, etc., then the present uncertainty at least is removed. What we observe is what there is, and there is then no question of delusion or over-all deception. We do not remove the latter if the identification with the bodily state is partial or indirect, as in Ayer's insistence that we are at least identified with our bodies in as much as, on his view, this is the only way we can ultimately speak of continued identity. So the 'middle way' does not help very much here. If mental states are not states of bodies there must be ways in which bodies mediate what is other than bodies, and here it is hard to avoid a theoretical possibility of being mistaken.

The proper reaction to this possibility is to recognise it

for what it is and take it in our stride as so remote as to cause neither practical nor philosophical anxiety. The evidence for taking some bodies to be animate is so overwhelming, the explanation in terms of sentience, thought and purpose is so obvious, and any evidence to the contrary so totally lacking, that we need have not the slightest qualms in dismissing our doubt. The worry to which Ayer draws attention is altogether bogus when we look it in the face. By interpreting our knowledge of one another in the way I have noted, that is in terms of what is the sensible explanation of what would otherwise be totally bewildering, we can extend our account to cases other than those of people being bodily present. Much of our communication does clearly take that form, most obviously in writing. We learn much, as has been intimated earlier, about people from signs or evidence which they have not contrived to produce for the purpose themselves. It is not the analogy with our own bodily states that is prominent here, if it is so anywhere, and such an analogy seems to be wholly absent if we think of possible communication with creatures about whose bodies we may know little or nothing.

In a case where there is no evidence of a particular body having been actually observed, if not by ourselves then by others at various removes in whom we may put some credence, there can be a difficult question as to whether one or more persons are involved. If a diary from some remote period comes to light and tells a fairly continuous story, then we can be fairly confident that it is the work of one man, though it may tell us about others. But in some such cases we might not be quite sure. We have similar uncertainties about the authorship of other books which do not bear so clearly the impress of one mind. We read of several 'Homers', a deutero-Isaiah etc. and wonder whether some or all of Shakespeare's plays were written by someone else, and how much of the Platonic dialogues tell us more about Socrates's mind than about Plato. In these cases we must make the best guess we can in the light of the evidence. Likewise, if we found ruins on a desert island we might wonder whether they are traces of one or more 'Robinson Crusoes'. One small hut suggests one person, a larger one perhaps more, and several huts certainly more. But we can not be quite sure. One survivor may have used several at different times. It might also prove difficult to know if signals from outer space come from one source or from several. We might have to leave it open or hazard the best guess the evidence allowed. Evidence of a continuous body with which the evidence could be linked would obviously help. But this is not indispensable, and we could in principle know a great deal about someone without evidence of any eye-witness or the like. We would normally, however, depend on some direct evidence.

This brings us very close to the question of a possible existence and fellowship with one another, without the sort of bodies we have now or perhaps of anything which could fairly be called a body. But, before we adventure further in that way, there is yet one other feature of our present involvement with our bodies which must be noted. Allusion has already been made to somatic sensations, the subtle sensations we have in our bodies fairly continuously without their being due to the more specific impact of other bodies. This has been thought by some to be the main source, or even the substance, of our sense of continued identity. That, on my view, is quite mistaken. But is seems clear, nonetheless, that the continuity of our experience is greatly assisted by the help thus given to our sense of continued bodily existence. How far this operates in dreams as well is a more difficult question, but the presumption is that we have the equivalent in some form in dreams.

Moreover, the body is in this, and a host of other related ways, the seat of a great deal that is tender and precious. It is not just like an old stick or a suit of clothes or a car or pipe to which we are very attached. It is not even like a house which has been someone's house all his life, so that he finds it hard to think of anyone else living there – it 'is a part of him'. We are never without our bodies, not even in dreams; for we dream of ourselves as we are when awake. We do not in fact just dwell in our bodies, and to speak in that way or declare that we are 'imprisoned' in the body, though quite appropriate for certain purposes, can also be very misleading; and, if we let ourselves be guided too closely by what we say, we end up, as has been pointed out, by failing to distinguish between mind and body. We express ourselves constantly, easily, spontaneously in our bodies, we do not contrive to manipulate them. I do not manufacture a smile, not even when I smile for the camera-man; I just smile, I beam my greeting to a friend or shrug another away, I scowl my disapproval. There is no part of my body which may not be immediately expressive in this and a host of other ways, every movement telling something, sometimes when I do not intend it. We blush and are sensitive because, when people look at our bodies, we feel they are looking at ourselves – *we* are comic or ridiculous or impressive as the case may be. We mirror our minds in our bodies and do this so constantly that we can think of people looking at us and looking into our souls. Tones of voice are equally expressive; we murmur our love or bark out the angry repartee. There is no noticeable interval, a fact which the behaviourist is so prone to exploit. My anger is not the shout, but the body is in this, and in an endless variety of ways, so constantly and readily expressive of what we are that we find it hard to think of ourselves without this unfailing and often unavoidable manifestation of our thoughts. This is why so many find it hard to avoid the identification of our thoughts with this constant articulation of them.

Even in the solitary 'sessions of sweet silent thought' the body often plays an important part, not just causally, but actively helping the thought or feeling along. An author may need to move around, to twiddle his thumbs or play with his pipe. He may need a special sort of pen or pencil and to slant the paper in a special way or have a particular chair or sit in a special position. Some think better 'on paper', others 'in their heads' or rumbling a speech in one's stomach, as has been said of one famous orator. We pucker the brow or tense ourselves in a special way, and this is not just to remove hindrances or distractions but as positive aids. Some have even said that they think or speak with the soles of their feet. The sound or gesture is itself formative of thought. We become thus peculiarly attached to our own bodies for their constant positive contribution to what we are and as a mirror of the soul, cracked and imperfect though it may be at times.

Much that is most precious may be sustained and disclosed in these ways. The smile or the tone of voice gives its character to love or hate. In particular there are physical sensations which have an exceptional place in expressing and furthering some of our finest and most intimate relationships. The caress is the obvious example. This may express deep affection, and in the manner of it may be induced, sustained and expressed a great deal of tenderness. At times it is appropriately casual, a playful pat on the back or a hug when the weary traveller gets home; sometimes it is more purposed and cultivated, at times enough so perhaps to defeat itself. A great deal depends on the persons involved and on the occasion, varying from the gentle pressure of a hand in sympathy to the giving and union of bodies in love. Just as rhyme and metre may at first appear an obstacle in poetry but are in fact welcomed, not as a constriction but as a means of liberation without which the work of genius could never come to be, so the constraints of our bodily states, even their imperfections, may also afford the means of a finer flowering of personal concern and expanding fellowship. Bodily contact has not a mean place in the right relationships, and for this reason the demeaning of it, in casual vulgarity or distortion, is an affront to the soul as well as the body. There can be an excessive concern with physical well-being and a one-sided preoccupation with physical delight. But it is at our peril that we live in this life as if the body had no place, or at best a very inferior one, in the most creative formative activities available to us and in the dearest and richest relationships we have. By contrast we should give better thought to the place it has and care for it as the medium of spiritual worth. It is not the soul alone that is holy.

This is where Plato made a great mistake. For he tended to place all bodily appetite and desire on a level. Hunger and thirst and physical fulfilment are the same for us as for brutes. In some regards they are, and we must not so 'elevate' or refine our appetites in our thoughts that they are not properly physical urges we share with lowlier creatures.

But Plato ranked them all on one side of our nature, in sharp isolation from reason, the real man. It is the function of reason to curb and tame. It is not that desire is evil, though we read in the *Republic* of unnecessary and even harmful desires. If allowed to grow out of proportion all desire is bad. The proper course is to keep our necessary appetites in their place and not encourage them to become wild by starving them. Total inhibition is foolish and Plato is wrongly thought of as a joyless ascetic. On the other hand, he held reason and desire too far apart in his famous tripartite division of the soul. Our physical desires are not just means of keeping soul and body effectively together as long as we have to in this world. They positively help one another. Reason is kept from operating in too rarefied a world of its own, and imagination is given its proper opportunity to body forth. Reason can thus permeate our desires, a much needed corrective which idealist followers of Kant also had to provide to Kant's excessive bifurcation of our nature into pure reason on the one hand and hedonistic desires on the other. When we eat we do not just satisfy brute appetite. Not even the brutes themselves do just that. They have some ritual and play of their own as they feed. We eat with our thoughts on other things as well – fitness, work, play; and there is a civilised way of eating for which the sauce is ceremony. Our desires may also be transformed and elevated, without surrender of what we mean by their so-called physical character or bodily origination, by the context in which they appear and are fulfilled. They are taken up into a richer universe of aims which modifies what they are in themselves; they are part of a rounded whole of living. In artistic experience, as in religion, they have a further range; what would either of these, as we know them, be without the body and physical existence? The body is thus not just an instrument for outward achievement or expression. It is a most important positive means of excellence, and it is this, as must also be stressed, because so much more than the body is involved.

Before very long the bodies of all who are living now will cease to function. They will decay or be reduced to ashes. If therefore, we are to entertain the possibility that we may in some form survive the dissolution of the body, which awaits us all, the question which first arises is whether, short of the resuscitation of our corpses which few would take seriously, we have to presuppose, in another life, some equivalent or analogue to our present bodies. In that case how close must the resemblance be? It is certainly easier for us to envisage an after life if we think of it as not altogether unlike the present one. We shall thus be provided with an environment of some kind, our experience will be focused and made precise, we shall have the equivalent of a body by which we are identified for one another and through which we communicate. Let us then now consider this possibility and ask ourselves how we can best understand the idea of a resurrection body.

8 The Resurrection World

It would seem that, over the ages, the greater part of mankind has believed in some kind of life after death. The position may be changing now, though for various reasons I doubt it. But there can be little doubt about the past. Most persons have lived in some expectation of being alive again after they are dead. This may not always have been a very 'real' expectation, in Newman's term; and that would account, in part, for the terror which death has often held for men – it would sometimes seem to be just 'the end'. But in the main this is not what seems to have prevailed. If we go by what people have professed, in their practices and culture especially, they seem to have had a fairly firm and sustained belief in some kind of destiny for themselves beyond their life in this world.

In most cases, moreover, men appear to have pictured what their life after death would be like, patterning it, as a rule, on what we find our present existence to be. Quite often life after death is envisaged as the kind of existence we have now, shorn of its most disagreeable features and with its more enjoyable aspects heightened or, when punishment is anticipated, with a terrible intensification of what we find most painful or distressing now. Men expect to go to 'happy hunting grounds' or to walk through Elysian Fields and taste the food and drink of gods or otherwise feast and enjoy themselves in the ways that delight them most now. Evil-doers will endure unspeakable and unrelieved agony in the fires of hell or drag out their misery in the muddy mire of Hades or performing dreary and frustrating tasks. How seriously these vivid pictures should be taken is a moot point. Professor C. H. Dodd is surely right in contending[1] that the vivid apocalyptic pictures we have in the Gospels and elsewhere in the New Testament were symbolic even for those who first composed or encountered them. Sometimes men have taken these pictures at their face value, and have literally thought of the graves and the seas yielding up their dead to be taken up into the clouds to meet their judge and redeemer. A literalist view of the Scriptures presumably requires this. But most of the time men in past ages, as today, had a shrewd sense of some things at least, in these contexts, being strictly metaphorical. On the other hand, while the place of metaphor was understood and respected, by naive as well as sophisticated persons, the 'other world' into which we passed at death, or after an appropriate interval, would be thought of most of the time on a very close analogy with the present one, the closeness of the analogy varying, even for the same person, according to mood and context.

For those who believe in reincarnation, the 'next life' will, in very many cases, be strictly the same as the present one; men come back to this world again. Many who hold this belief entertain also the expectation that eventually, when their Karma, for example, is duly discharged, they will be released from any kind of bodily existence, and indeed from all particularity. But in the meantime there are many lives like the present one to be lived. These present the problems already noted. For the present my concern is not mainly with after-life lived out in the present world, or somewhere in the universe of space and time as we know it now, but with another 'world' which is in no way continuous with the physical universe that we now inhabit, but which is like it in important respects and in which we can, without too great a strain on our terms, be said to have an embodied existence. We shall not have physical bodies, but nevertheless bodies sufficiently like our present ones to be thought of and described in the same terms.

One of the most ingenious attempts to proceed in this way, and thus to form a fairly precise picture of what 'the next world' must be like, is that of Professor H. H. Price in a justly celebrated Presidential Address to The Society for Psychical Research in 1952. This has since been reproduced, with comments by other writers, in a volume entitled *Brain and Mind* edited by J. R. Smythies. This address

was entitled 'Survival and the Idea of "Another World" '.
Variations on a similar theme are played by Professor John
Hick in his article 'Theology and Verification' in *Theology
Today*, April 1960. Both of these papers have been much
discussed since their publication, and this reflects an inter-
esting renewal of interest in this kind of speculation.

The main clue for Price is found in the fact of dreams. We
all do dream, and in a dream we seem to enter an entirely
different world, but, at the same time, a world which is very
similar in many respects to the world of waking consciousness. Much the same sort of thing happens in dreams as in
waking life. Suppose that I dream of being on a picnic in the
New Forest. I seem to see grass and trees and the odd pony
much as I normally would, I help to carry the food to a
quiet spot, I chat with my friends. In dreams the continuity
is sometimes abruptly broken, but for slices of our dreams
at least there seems to be little to differentiate overtly between them and normal experience. We seem to see, touch,
or hear things in the same way, and we behave, in essentials
very much as we normally do. This is why we are, as a rule,
completely taken in. There are, it appears, some occasions,
usually today called 'lucid dreams', when people are aware
at the time that they are dreaming. But this is rare, except
perhaps for periods just before falling properly asleep or
waking. This, in addition to the intensity of many dreams,
is why they leave us with a sense of great delight or terror,
according to the kind of dream it is. We take it all very
seriously and sometimes find it hard to shake off when we
are awake.

At the same time we also say, 'But of course it never
happened. It was not real, it was just a dream, it is gone
for ever'. We are relieved when we wake up to find that
some appalling thing that seemed to happen was just a
nightmare, although at the time it was real enough for us
to be terrified and even tumble about and perspire in our
actual physical body. The trees in my dream of the picnic
are not real trees. No other trees were cut to make room
for them, they took no time to grow, and, even though we
may count the rings on a stump, this will not give them a
real age. No one else will see them, and, even though we

speak of 'entering' the world of my dreams, I do not strictly enter it, at least not in the sense in which I pass through
a door to enter a garden. I do not pass in this sense to the
world of my dream; I do not travel to the New Forest of my
dream, nor could anyone say how far it is from my home to
this dream forest. The real New Forest is about forty miles
from my home, but the forest in my dream is not forty miles
away, nor ten nor a hundred, nor any other distance. It is
just pointless to ask how far it is, and that is not because it
is exceptionally hard to measure or to discover, as one
might find it hard to locate some barely penetrable spot in
the Amazonian jungle. We are now beginning to explore
outer space, and there may be places which men may, in
fact, never be able to reach even in relays, or bodies which
recede faster than any conceivable means of travel. But
these cases are quite different from the impossibility of
locating or literally entering the New Forest of my dream.
The latter is not in physical space at all. It is private and
not in any public space.

No one would deny this. And yet, in some sense, the trees
in my dream are in space. They are not wholly unreal. Admittedly some would say that the entities which fill my
dream are not real in any sense, any more than other
mental images. I can imagine my house being on fire, but
there is no fire. But here we need to distinguish, as Price
does, between imagining in the broad sense and imaging.
The former might involve nothing more than taking something to be the case in thought, or supposing or pretending
or acting as if something were other than it is. But I can
also image or visualise my house being ablaze. In this case
I conjure up an image. In the case of hallucinations the
image can, in fact, be located. Macbeth saw his famous
dagger 'before' him, 'the handle towards my hand'. He
knew exactly where the ghost of Banquo had taken his
seat. This is what, in some sense, he saw, and if we like to
say that 'seeing' and 'touching' can only refer to actual
physical entities, the reply can be made, firstly that we
might be legislating contrary to actual linguistic practice
(Macbeth said he *saw* and so would most people over a
long tradition of talking about hallucinations, mirages,

dreams and latterly films and television), and secondly, that whatever may be the proper or accepted linguistic convention, the fact remains that Macbeth would have an experience identical in some respects with seeing a dagger – there would be something presented to him. It may be the creation of his fevered brain, and I only see my house ablaze in dreams. But the dream flames are not in my brain, and I do not dream of looking into my brain. I seem to stand on the lawn and there are the flames bursting out of the roof and up into the sky. The experience is as close in essentials at the time to actual seeing as any could be. I do not dream of pretending but of seeing my house ablaze.

This is peculiarly evident in the case of perspectival distortion as of hallucinations, and this is why we can actually place those in physical space. I can say where exactly I see the proverbial pink rat. It is there 'at the foot of the bed' or 'on the mantelpiece'. I can point exactly to what I see in a mirror and even take it to be real people in a room; I can shoot an arrow through a reflection in the water. The location of an after-image is not in doubt. This is because the images, in these cases, do stand in a firm relation to actual entities in space. The pink rat is just at the corner of the mantelpiece, I can say exactly where it is; the 'dagger' could come to rest on the table and its outline might even be drawn. We are less inclined to say this of a mental image or of what we see in a dream. But even here it might not be so completely out of the question as might at first appear. A person with a capacity for very vivid imaging might actually conjure up deliberately the image of a spoon at his place on the table. Other persons do not see this spoon and he himself cannot eat with it. There might even be some kind of actual location for the mental images which others of us, less gifted in this way, conjure up. We tend to distance them in some measure from where we are and to have them in a certain direction, determined partly by psychological factors or events of our own history. If I conjure up a picture of my own college I place it to my left, for that is the direction where London and the college lie. This gives us very little precision, and it may be that not a great deal hangs on this point. In dreams we have not the concurrent apprehension of the world around us, and no way of placing things except where they are in the dream.

The fact that we are able to place our images in some relation to actual entities in space raises some exceptionally difficult questions about the nature of space, and it may point to some very unexpected conclusions. I was much concerned with some of these questions in a paper I read to the Aristotelian Society some years ago[2]. I pointed out, for example, that if we find that we have to accord some real depth to what we see in a mirror or in some other way give them a location, however temporary, then there is the question of the displacement of the entities which other people perceive in the same place, and I suggested that this might have the implication that we all have initially our private spaces, but that what such spaces are like must differ radically, as features of people's actual experience, in their nature from one case to another. There would still be a common factor out of which our understanding of public space would be built up, mainly through correlations between our experiences. But what space as experienced would be like would be radically different for each of us, as, in a less drastic way, colours might not be strictly the same as each of us actually experiences them. Some may recall here also Spinoza's doctrine of infinite attributes.

At this point we come to the edges of some unusually abstruse and complicated problems. But fortunately we do not have to go deeper into them for our purpose. What matters most for us is that images, whether in waking consciousness or in dreams, have some kind of spatial quality. Even where there is no possibility, as normally happens in dreams, of relating the image to the real or external world in any way at all, there is extendedness and positioning of objects, whatever their status is taken to be, within the dream appearance itself. I use 'appearance' rather than 'world' here, for the flames that devour my house in my present nightmare stand in no ascertainable spatial relation to the river on whose banks I was fishing in an earlier dream, although with ingenuity we might find something intelligible to say even here. But within a particular dream as it occurs everything has its location; there is the door of my house *in front* of me where I stand in the middle of the lawn, the window to the *right* of it, the *sloping* roof *above*, and so on. The flames shoot *up* into the sky and the flying sparks alight alarmingly on trees further away in the garden, men run along with buckets and hose-pipes, all having their place in the picture as they move. This seems beyond denial, unless the bold and, to my mind, preposterous, step is taken of denying that we do picture things in this lively way in dreams or, with Professor Malcolm, that anything at all goes on[3]. The experience in the dream is as near to seeing as anything can be. This is what most persons would say. Indeed, from very long ago people have spoken of what they *saw* in a dream, not merely of pretending or behaving as if certain things were happening.

Now Price's suggestion is that we may think of 'the next world' as an image world, very like the world of our dreams, but with the additional feature of a more comprehensive and complete correlation of the images involved. The 'other' world would, in fact, be a world. It would have stability and system, though by no means in the same way, and not perhaps with the same exhaustiveness, as the world of nature we inhabit now. There would be tactual as well as visual images, auditory images and smell images too. There would be images of organic sensations, including somatic sensations connected with the images that would make up one's own body. 'Such a family of inter-related images would make a pretty good object.[4]' The rules relating such images, or the objects which a family of them might constitute, might not be the same as the laws of nature in the present world. We might find, for instance, that what we would normally (or now) take to be impenetrable objects could be passed through without damage, as we now immerse ourselves in water. There might be causation at a distance, and the other properties of our own bodies might be different, conditions could be more lax, or more severe, in some respects. It could in some ways be like the world of magic or fairy land. But it could not be this without limit. There would have to be some fairly firm consistency, for an image world in which everything changed at random would not be a world in which anything could be recognised or in which intelligent functioning would be possible. The rules would be different; they might be more flexible, but there would have to be rules.

There are indeed sharp variations within the world as we know it now – altitude makes a difference to the degree at which water boils, and in outer space things are weightless. But all this is also closely correlated to what we find in different conditions close to the earth. It is not a random change but one which can be understood and anticipated, as scientists do today with remarkable skill. Science is possible because the world of nature remains one world. We make sense of the variations, microscopic and macroscopic alike, on this assumption, and if we are defeated by what appears to be some quite mad behaviour at times, we still look for some method in the madness. It must make sense somehow; and if there should be thought to be some random behaviour on occasion in the world of nature, this could certainly not be the rule if science, and indeed ordinary day-to-day existence, are to be possible.

The 'other world' would differ in the kind of rules that hold, and in the modes of their operation. It might not be so close-knit a world as this one. But why regard it as strictly another world, why not some part of this one in which things behaved oddly, as in outer space? The main reason for this would be the total lack of continuity or causal relation with the world we know now. This is anticipated already in the case of mental images and other appearances which we would not normally take to be 'real'. A shadow is cast on a real surface by my real body, but it does not have permanent effects like a smear of paint, and we say 'it is just a shadow', though in this case located in the world of nature. The pink rat of my delirium has no antecedent in the external world, other than my fevered brain (and whatever caused that). It may owe much directly to my state of mind. But it leaves no trace once it has gone and I am well again; the edge of the mantel-piece has not been gnawed. It is all as if nothing had happened. This is what we mainly mean when we say that it was not a real rat. It was, while it lasted, as much 'an actual entity', in Price's words, 'as real as anything can be'. But it was 'wild', in the sense in which philosophers use this word in discussing perception. It stood in no continuous ascertainable relation to other entities. It was not produced as other things are, it is not killed by poison, it could not return except by a like delirium, and if it did it would just be there out of nowhere. It is not seen by others. No one can catch it and keep it in a cage.

In the case of the other *world*, the break with causal continuity is total, or as total as makes no difference. The images involved affect one another and thus constitute objects, including bodies of our own, which we can identify and manipulate, but which have no effect, or at least not normally, on our presentations of the present world of nature and whatever further external reality may be thought to account for these. They are like the pink rat, as far as this world is concerned; it is as if they had never been. I say 'normally', for, while it is generally assumed that the dead do not return, there are claims made on occasion that the dead do communicate with the living and even appear or materialise in this world. This could have various forms. One would be an immediate impact on the mind, as in telepathy in this life. This involves no intersecting of the presented worlds themselves; it is as between mind and mind, although this could have repercussions in turn, in the normal way, on the external world if it produces some physical reaction on our part. But the departed are thought sometimes to communicate with us, as in mediumistic séances by inducing some change in our present environment, causing the table to rap or the pencil to move. They may also appear as ghosts. In the latter case the intersecting is slight, though it may have momentous consequences as in Hamlet. The ghost itself does not do anything, beyond being seen and uttering certain sounds. It does not, for example, move things or open a hole through which to emerge which remains afterwards for all to inspect. It is, however, allegedly seen by many persons and has some kind of momentary place in our space. It has this very partially if nothing is disturbed and if it is purely visual and passes through walls without damage to them. That is how ghosts are normally thought to behave. But a poltergeist does sometimes move things around and damage them. In that case it seems to get firmly out of its own space into ours. On the other hand, its normal habitat is the other world, and what I think we must say is that the image world which the dead, on the present supposition, inhabit has its own system and completeness which does not involve the causal course of events in this world except very intermittently and in limited peripheral ways. Otherwise we could not easily regard it as a properly different world with a different space.

Much will turn also on how the denizens of the other world are supposed to make their occasional impact on this one. Have they in their turn, for instance, to make certain moves in the image world of their own space, corresponding to our sitting round a table and holding hands, before they get through? We are sometimes told of departed 'subjects' finding it difficult to 'get through', and Price has ascribed the oddity of some of the purported messages to this difficulty. Is this difficulty one which only affects our side of the transaction, or are there requisite undertakings on the 'other side' which may not always be easy to fulfil? If the latter involve not just mental concentration or attainment of some kind but the manipulation of the image entities of the other world, or the maintenance of some posture of such bodies as they have there, then the one world is not so completely cut off from the other as we suppose in first entertaining the present supposition. It is not quite so unlike communication with outer space as we are first inclined to think. On the other hand, the *modus operandi* of the image entities of the world beyond is so completely at variance with the causal relations we establish in this one, and the impact of the one on the other so rare and peripheral (and as far as the external order of things is concerned non-existent directly) that the best sense we can make of it is to regard it as having an 'order of nature' of its own quite distinct from this one. Holding hands in a séance has not much in common with exploring outer space.

An additional complication, when we try to think how we should conceptualise the idea of another world in the present terms, is that while we are not, to our knowledge, able

to affect the state of things directly in the other world and
have no proper notion of how things function there, it is
sometimes supposed that the dead are not subject to the
same limitations regarding us. I mean that it is sometimes
thought that the dead can not only break through with
communications in some way on rare occasions to us, and
even effect material change 'here below', but that they are
also fairly continuously apprised of what goes on here, at
least in some area – they observe us, although we are quite
unable to observe them except in the rare form of appari-
tions in this world. We do not peer into the world of the
dead at all, but they perhaps peer at us. Indeed some spir-
itualists suppose that the 'departed', and other spirits perhaps, are about us all the time, or at least can be present
and aware of what goes on very much as we do in perception. How is this supposed to happen?

One answer would be that the dead are not strictly in a
world of their own, as in Price's present supposition. They
really do have bodies like our own which are causally affected, as our bodies are and in ways which are in principle
detectable by us, by our present physical environment.
These are 'subtle' bodies, and they cannot be perceived by
us, or at least not normally. They are affected by stimuli
from the same physical world as ourselves, though the
means by which they perceive them may be different. It is a
bit like the conjuror who makes himself (or others) invisible
with mirrors while being all the time properly there unseen
by us. The substance of the subtle body is such that it does
not, in fact, get through to us in the normal stimulation of
our sense organs. But it is itself affected, in subtle ways perhaps though presumably with some kind of sense organs,
by the same physical reality as affects our eyes and ears. In
that case the dead are not strictly in another world. They
are in this one in a very special way.

In that case it should be possible, in principle, to detect
the presence of such spirits in some scientific way. It may be
exceptionally difficult to do this, but it is hard to see what
difficulty in principle there is in making the 'subtle' body
yield up its secret. The more sceptical amongst us will also
dwell on the absence of any indication of such subtle

influences in the kind of physical situation with which we
are normally familiar – should they not have made themselves felt in some fashion? There are others, however, who
will not be daunted by this thought and who will remind us
of the many properties and energies of the material world
which give no evidence of themselves in our normal perception of the world but have been made manifest for the first
time in extremely sophisticated scientific studies in our own
day. Who would dream of atomic energy by just looking at
things?

If it is held, however, that the subtle body is, in principle,
incapable of any kind of scientific detection by us, we are
back with the more self-contained image world with a space
of its own. If the inhabitants of this world observe us they
do not do so by normal perception. We are left then with
two main choices. We may take our cue from occurrences
like telepathy and suppose that the dead become aware of
what goes on in this world without any media of any kind or
by some mode of apprehension of which we can form no
conception. This would leave the matter, as far as we are
concerned, an almost total mystery. Or we may suppose
that, in a way that takes no account of the causal conditions
that hold in this world, certain features or combinations of
events in the quite distinct image world of the dead mirror
for them the events of this world, or some of them.
Presumably the dead are not aware of all that goes on in
this world. There must be some selection and focusing of
the kind to which they were accustomed in this life. That
must indeed occur equally within their own world if chaos
is to be avoided; and what other purpose could a space
and bodies serve? What we must suppose, therefore, is,
not that the dead acquire immediately, or indeed at any
stage, some kind of omniscience about the world they
have left, but that they are able, in a selective way consistent with the kind of beings they were initially, to have
awareness of some things in the present world through
certain features of the images which present themselves in
the new one.

We would expect that memories of the world they left
behind, and the general sense of what it was like, would

be very important for any apprehension by the dead of anything that occurs in this world now. I shall note this question of memory again. But if we allow it, we can have at least a better idea of how some disposition of things in the next world could be found intelligible only on the assumption that events in the present world do reflect themselves in some way in the patterns of some events in the 'next' one. The dead might thus come to have what is for them an experience of observing what is happening to us, at least in limited ways, and try, on this basis, as mediums claim they do, to communicate with us. In the absence of a clearer notion than we have now, or are ever very likely to have, of what kind of image or quasi-perceptual world the dead may be supposed to inhabit, it is well-nigh impossible for us to work out in any detail how any influence of one world on the other, and any communication between them, is possible. We can only console ourselves, if the question troubles us, with the reflection that perception, and the mediated communication we have with one another now, are also very remarkable and much more extraordinary than we realise in our day-to-day habituation to them in common experience. There are, however, questions, intriguing and tantalising, about space and a possible embodiment in another existence which have not been tackled, or even formulated, with the precision and boldness which we must expect from those who entertain this possibility as part of their consideration of a possible future existence.

Price himself gives us only the main clues for his construction of a possible other world, or 'the next world'. He is characteristically modest and tentative about it. But he does advance fairly boldly the view that the composition of the 'next world' will be affected a great deal more than the present world by our own wishes. One reason for this is that dreams, which are much the best model we have of the kind of life which Price envisages here, seem to be much affected by our wishes and main preoccupations, including repressed desires of whose importance we have learnt much from Freud. Price does not find this in all ways a comforting thought. Some of our most powerful desires, including shameful ones which we now suppress or control, might not be the best determinants of a new environment for us; but we might be getting the 'next world' that we deserve, and Price finds an obvious affinity of his own suggestion here with much of the teaching of Hindu thinkers about 'a world of desire'. If there is substance in this, it is certainly a sobering thought for us in the present life. One may recall Plato's description of the last stage of degeneration of the tyrannical man when 'he becomes always and in waking reality what he was then', that is when his desires 'were only let loose in the dreams of sleep', 'very rarely and in a dream only'[5]. A world of unrepressed desires could become a terrible world.

I do not see, however, why the usefulness of the analogy of dreams, for the construction of an image world distinct from present material reality, should require us to give this prominence to our own desires in the determination of our next world. Our desires do undoubtedly affect our dreams, both those we have when properly asleep and our daydreams. This is not surprising, for the main thing we have here is the removal of the awkward restraints of waking experience in the world of nature. But the next world would not just be one where awkward restraints were removed. It would not be just a dream where the major part could be played by our own hopes and fears. It would need to be a *world*. And here we have to note that there could be two ways in which the next world could be fashioned on the basis of our own desires. It might be that anything and everything we wished for would instantly appear, and there would be nothing to which we were averse. It would be a world of Aladdin's lamp and magic. But if it were wholly this it would be chaotic. There would have to be some rules even in the wildest games we play in our dreams, and fairly firm rules if there is to be continuity. So the next world would certainly not be just a world of instant desire. On the other hand, we may suppose by contrast that desire becomes the fashioner of the next world in the sense that the main drive of our own desires, or their general tone and quality, set the main conditions of the world we are to enter. It is generally after our heart's desire. But the difficulty here, and the point where the analogy of dreams cannot be pressed, is that it is supposed to be also in some way a public world. If there is no necessity about the world I am to enter, how can there be any correlation between it and the worlds of other subjects? There must be some common restraints if communication is to be possible. Otherwise the next world will be a nightmarish, solipsistic one. The general expectation is that fellowship will be even more important, and more complete and adequate, in the next world. That is one reason for looking forward to it and for much of the kind of preparation we are exhorted to undertake. The Christian thinks of it as a completer attainment of the Kingdom of God than is possible now. But, in that case, it cannot be a world fashioned too completely according to subjective predilections. It must be a world in which close communication is possible.

This does not mean that our lot in another world could not be much affected by what we have become or made of ourselves in this one; and that, I imagine, is what Professor Price has mainly in mind. That would be in line with much that happens already here. We may ruin our lives by the way we live, and it could be said, in that case, that we have brought our fate on ourselves. By contrast life may become richer because we have cultivated certain gifts of mind or character. We may enter the next life very ill-equipped for it, or we may already have acquired much that is to count there. But this concerns the lot we have in another world, the way we fare there, not the media or conditions by which it is possible. How those are determined is quite another point. But if we are thinking, as we are at present, in terms of some embodiment not altogether unlike our present physical existence, our initial consideration must be the sort of conditions which would make it possible for it to be a genuine *world* in which communication with others takes place; and at this point there does not seem to be much place for our own desires. The next world, if there is one, will be what it will be irrespective of our own desires. We have no reason to suppose that we shall fashion it, any more than we make our present world. Or, if this is not the case, we need strong metaphysical or religious arguments for such a view other than the place of our own wishes in the very private imaging of our hallucinations and dreams. Our dreams may be very much our own. It is very unlikely that the next world will be. And that is a sobering thought as well.

A further point made by Price is that speculative thinkers like Schopenhauer or Berkeley, to whose views strong objections might be taken as accounts of present physical reality, may nonetheless be found to have triumphed in another way, that is by giving a 'substantially correct' account of the next world. I do not quite go with this. I do not see why Berkeley, for example, could not be right about both worlds. The question of whether we should think of the external world as involving some order of nature distinct from the necessity and coherence of the world as we experience it, is a difficult one. But if we take our cue, in thinking of the next world, from Berkeley, it does not follow that there would not be important, indeed quite radical, differences, between a Berkeleyan *next* world and the present physical world as Berkeley understood it. The major difference would be in the rules which operated in the two worlds; and it is hard to see what argument brought against a Berkeleyan view of the external world, or any subsequent phenomenalist variation upon it, would not require also the postulation of some distinct external system to account for the continuity and order of appearances in another image world. The issue of a causal theory of perception appears to be neutral so far as Price's ingenious account of a possible next world is concerned.

The crux, however, for most philosophers, when they consider Price's present view, comes over the question of identity. How would anyone know who he was himself, or who anyone else was (or had been before), if he found himself in Price's image world? This is the point that has been most stressed in comments on Professor Hick's variation on the theme of Price's paper. Hick invites us[6] to consider these cases. A person suddenly disappears from a room in America and immediately appears in Australia. In all respects the person who is now seen in Australia is similar to the one who vanished in America. In all testable physical detail he is similar; he remembers what happened before the change and responds appropriately to erstwhile friends who are sent to interview him. Nothing is at odds with normal expectation except the fact that, instead of travelling from Princeton to Melbourne, the man now in Melbourne just found himself there the moment he stopped being in Princeton. We would, Hick contends, have no doubt that it was the same man in both cases. Likewise, in the second case, where we are to suppose that the man in Princeton has died and his corpse is there to be examined, buried or cremated. A man exactly like him appears at once in Melbourne. We would again say that it was the same person in the two cases. The circumstances are remarkable, but, Hick maintains, conceivable. Why not, then, extend this further and suppose that the dead person finds himself reconstituted in another world with a space of its own. We cannot send a deputation this time, but the dead person has his own memories and character traits, and he meets acquaintances and friends whom he knows to be dead. He would now know that he had been reconstituted in another world.

These are Hick's cases. One question which arises here at once is how would a person know that he and others he met were in a strictly different *world* and not in some remote and perhaps, in practice, inaccessible part of ordinary space. Hick does not deal with this, but just refers us to considerations reflected in the Lukan reference to 'a great gulf fixed'¹. This is not, to my mind, adequate here. For while it might be appropriate to say that, in a religious context, we may have good reasons to affirm things about an after-life which we cannot wholly explain, an attempt to further the case by indicating what our reconstituted existence would be like would seem to require that more be said on the question just raised. What, in fact, would be the gulf fixed between existence in one sort of space and in another? I have, however, touched on this already, and, as I have not more to add on this score, let us take the question that seems to have worried readers more, namely how would someone, in the third case instanced, know that he was the person who had just died. And how would others know it?

I must first note that the words '*just* died' have no special importance in this case. They have not, in fact, in the other case, except incidentally as making us more convinced that there is no trickery. If I appear in Australia the moment I die or vanish, then the likelihood of fraud or the acquisition in some other way of the physical and mental characteristics of my double seems more remote. The application of obvious tests would be easier and more complete. In other ways the lapse of time would not matter much. If the facts could be equally firmly established, the main issues would remain the same. If someone with my finger-prints and apparently having my memories, etc., appeared five years after I had vanished or died, the present reasons for declaring him to be me would remain. In the case of the 'next' world the precise point of 'just' might also be queried. But let us, nonetheless stick to the central question. Granted these peculiar situations how is a person identified?

One critic[8] has urged that, if God could reconstitute a person out of some material other than physical matter and locate him in 'a resurrection world', he might create many such persons, and how could it ever be said that one of them, and not the others, was the one who had lived and died in this world? Presumably such persons could be distinguished from one another, for they would occupy different parts of the space of the resurrection world. But if they were similar in all other ways, how could it ever be known that one of them was our acquaintance in *this* world?

The problem here does not seem to me substantially different from the one that presented itself earlier in the case of reincarnations in the present existence; and, if the views I have put forward earlier hold, substantially the same thing may be said to take the sting out of difficulties in the one case as in the other. In the first place, the person himself will know, in the basic sense noted earlier, that he is the person he finds himself to be and no other. He will know himself as one being who could not be another, however his characteristics or appearances may change. He will know this as true of himself, even if he fails to reflect upon it or express it adequately, even if he has no remembrance of a previous existence in which he was, and would have to be, the same being. But he may also have memories, or it may be some other knowledge, of his former life; and in that case his identity, in the sense of continued identity with the person known to have existed otherwise, is also established – for him and for any who can be made aware of the facts.

But, it will be argued, memory presents a peculiarly intractable problem in the present supposition. For how could there possibly be any check on our memories of existence in a totally different world? If the 'great gulf' is fixed such that there is no coming and going, if our world has now 'a space of its own', how could it ever be shown that our memories are genuine? In reply let it first be recalled that I have indicated how, in principle, there could be the sort of traffic between this world and the next which mediums, for example, claim and how, in the case of the dead, this could be more complete, on their side, for reasons affecting the mode of their existence which are unknowable to us. It may be that they can check their memories in some measure. They may also check them with one another, though this will not wholly meet Mr Clarke's point. But it has also been urged earlier that the confidence we have in our memories does not depend entirely on our ability to check them. We seem able to place reliance upon them in and for themselves; and if this holds in the present existence, why not in another? If I find reason to believe some day that I have passed from my present existence to another but seem also to recall the kind of thing that I would normally recall at present, should I really doubt that it is a genuine memory of the things that have happened in the present life and what it was like? It may be that God has created me anew with a wholly illusory impression of all this. But I have no reason to suspect this. It is not in accord with what I expect, any more than I am led to doubt in any similar way the explicit memories I have now, deceptive though some seeming memories may be. I have certainly no reason to suspect that a demon is playing a game with me. And why should I suspect this in another world?

'But', Mr Clarke or someone of like mind will say, 'what

of the disconcerting situation where there appear in the
next world several persons who have my appearance, memories and other characteristics, who are in all respects
similar except for the relatively trivial item of their location?' To this, in principle, I say the same as I would if such
doubles of someone now dead appeared in this world. In
the first place, only one of these pretenders (and possibly
none) would be the person who had lived before on earth.
Only one set of alleged memories would be genuine memories, though the others, however ensured, would be equally true to the facts. In the second place, memory being
what it is, we may perhaps, in our concern to be fair and
concede all we can, admit too readily the reasonableness of
the supposition that more than one person may have seemingly the same strict memories. There seem to be no clear
instances of this, though many other strange things are
claimed. But even if this curious situation did come about,
it would not affect the substance of what is at issue about
our identity. It would be gravely disconcerting in practice
but no more.

If, for example, I found myself in this situation in the next
world, I would know who I was myself and would trust the
substance of my memories to the extent of taking them to
establish my identity with the person I remembered as
myself in my past life. I would leave it open what would
account for there seeming to be other persons in just the
same situation. It would be awkward when other people
would have no means of coming to a like adjudgment between us, as there could be embarrassment in other ways
where the similarities are so complete. I would assume that
I was the victim of some evil mischance, and that since God
had allowed or intended this he had some compensating
purpose in mind, as in the case of other evils which baffle
us. I would have to make the best of the situation while it
lasted. Other people would apparently have no means of
judging which, if any, was the genuine claimant, and they
might find it very hard to know which of the many doubles
was the one who did this or that at some other 'time' in the
new world.

The latter situation is no more than a peculiarly acute

extension of situations in which we may find ourselves in the present life when confronted with identical twins. As the authors of detective stories know only too well, the existence of identical twins and doubles lead to baffling complications. If God chooses to confront us with some extraordinary variation on this in the next life, so be it. It is in accordance with his will as are other sore trials. At the same time there appears to be no reason why God should act in this way, and as we have reason to suppose that the next life, even if not the final change of its kind, will take us out of the evils that dog us now, we would not normally expect to be confronted with a major aggravation of one of these evils in the next life. The reasons we have for believing in such a life may fairly firmly preclude that. It seems, therefore, very unlikely that circumstances like those envisaged, very properly for this purpose, by Mr Clarke, will in fact come about. But it is also worth remembering that we could be mystified, even in the present life, by some turn of events which shares some of the perplexities Mr Clarke envisages. Suppose, for example, that mirrors were introduced for the first time to a society where they had not been known and where perhaps there were no reflections of any kind. If several persons, in that situation, entered a room lined with mirrors of which they had no previous experience, they would be thrown into complete confusion, and it would take some time to sort it out. But there would be a perfectly satisfactory explanation. One would go on in similar hopes if a like fate befell some of us in another life.

It must now be added that, while it is important and interesting to consider how we might picture or understand another existence in the terms that are familiar to us now, that is in terms of images that give us an embodiment not very unlike the physical existence we have in this world, we have no reason to suppose that this is the only possibility. There could indeed be many varieties within the sort of other world we construct out of present experience. Some of our present senses, or their equivalent in the image world, might be differently related to others. Some might not have the prominence they have now, or they might be replaced or supplemented by some other sense. But we might also find ourselves functioning in some entirely different mode of which we have no conception now, or in a totally disembodied state.

It may be worth asking more closely, however, how the latter should be understood.

9 The World of Thoughts Alone

By disembodied existence I mean, in the present context, two things. Firstly, that we shall not have a body like the present physical body or *be* in any other way in the present order of nature. Secondly, we shall have nothing strictly analogous to our present bodies, for example image bodies of the kind already considered. We shall have no world or environment in the ordinary sense. There will be only thoughts, or a world of thoughts, and appropriate mental reactions to them. This is not how the word 'disembodied' is always understood. But I shall be using it here in the sense indicated. No one finds it easy to think of this kind of totally disembodied being. It is very hard to divest ourselves in imagination of the conditions to which we are fully habituated now, especially when so many find it hard to think at all without some imaged accompaniment. Even a world of thoughts, or the idea of a thought or thought process, comes before us in the guise of some image. But we may at least get close to our quarry in this way, namely by thinking of occasions when we are very deep in thought on some abstract topic and oblivious, as we say, of the world around us. It is not always of such a theme that we are thinking when 'lost' in thought. We may have very deep reveries of another sort, in a very vivid day-dream about one's visit abroad perhaps or the next game of tennis. But I am now supposing that we are not imaging anything of that sort but following out a highly abstract train of thought, like trying to solve a problem in arithmetic or algebra or attempting some new variation on the ontological argument for the existence of God. Some people are much better than others at doing this without the aid of images and, so they say, can dispense with the need for images entirely.

In such cases, no one is wholly oblivious of his body, or at least this is what we normally presume. Some mystics may offer an exception, but that is a very special case with problems of its own. Most of us, when deep in thought, do retain some consciousness of our environment. We are not quite unaware of where we are; we have some bodily sensations from the chair on which we sit or the floor on which our feet are resting. There will be somatic sensations 'within' our bodies. Some of these may drop into what psychologists have sometimes called the margin of consciousness or of attention – or perhaps into some kind of unconscious or sub-conscious. But we are not wholly without them; we are not bodiless. But let us now suppose that the body is actually whisked away or just disappears, and with it all our physical environment. Let us assume that our preoccupation is such that we do not notice this; and we are not concerned at the moment with the causal question, but with what is conceivable. It is hard to believe that this strange event could happen without a shock that would disturb our train of thought. Nonetheless, we do become at times astonishingly oblivious of what goes on around us; and what I am asking now is that we carry this further and suppose us to continue with just the train of thought that is holding our attention now. That would continue in time, but without space of any kind.

Some might object that this is, in fact, not conceivable. For space and time, they hold, go together, indeed that what we have is a space-time continuum. I shall not pause to consider here what this last term really means. I doubt very much whether it means anything outside a very special context in physics. It is easily bandied about. All I will say now is that the situation I have just described seems perfectly intelligible. It is a continuation of what in fact largely happens, and I submit that there is no overwhelming problem about the conceivability of our continuation in the bodiless state I have just noted. We would not be aware of what has happened. The content of our thought would be wholly the train of thought that absorbs us.

This, it will be said, is conceivable; but what is not conceivable is that we should really exist or continue to function in a world of thoughts alone as suggested. To continue for a while, on the momentum of our present thought, is one thing; to be functioning solely in that way is quite another, not for the causal reasons which are not strictly relevant here, but as a matter of conceivability. One reason for this is the supposition that even very abstract ideas, like those of arithmetic or algebra, presuppose something of a spatial nature and can only be acquired through the experience we have had of the presented world over against us. This is a very large issue, and I cannot go here into the cluster of very difficult questions about universals. Let it be enough for the present to say that I do not find the suggestion just made about our knowledge of universals too daunting; nor do I consider it crucial for the points at issue now. We may, in fact, have acquired our understanding of universals in the course of our experience of a given particularised world, though that in itself could not, in my view, be taken without qualification. But I see no reason in principle why we could not have thoughts of non-bodily things in another way, and that even we might have some thought of the actual world of nature without experience of it, as God must have had – if we entertain the idea of God. There seems certainly no reason to suppose that, once such notions are acquired, we can not continue to entertain them, including thoughts (though not *ex hypothesi* images) of the physical world where it began for us, even in the disembodied state under discussion now.

Harder problems arise in other ways, and it is these that a critic will be most concerned to stress. How, it will be asked, can we have any sense of identity in such a world of thoughts? Would there not just be the passing thought? What reference could there be for anything else or ourselves? This is a point much stressed by Professor Peter Strawson in his chapter on 'Monads' in *Individuals*. There would be no way of placing a thought, he contends, or regarding it as this thought occurring now. It would be indiscernible from other similar thoughts, and so we would have to pay

a very high price: the price, namely, of acknowledging that the individuals of the system are not particulars at all, but universals or types or concepts. It is, perhaps, a price that a mathematically-minded metaphysician is quite willing to pay[1].

As it is also put, it would be a severely 'Platonistic' world[2]. There would be no particulars.

I find this somewhat perplexing. Strawson himself, in his earlier chapter on 'Sounds', has tried to work out how we might have appropriate contrasts and discriminate enough to give us some kind of placing and a genuine environment in a world of sounds but no other sense. He does not claim that such a world is possible, except as a model 'against which to test and strengthen our own reflective understanding of our own conceptual structure'[3]; and, for reasons unfolded in the chapter on 'Persons', it seems plain that Strawson would not entertain the idea of a purely auditory world as a seriously possible one. But he does work out ingeniously how, in terms of varying pitch-range and a master-sound, we might find some way to identify particulars in a world of sound. We might even 'open the door to something like communication'[4], if we supposed further that some changes might be initiated and a distinction drawn 'between changes that are brought about and changes that merely occur', and thus, 'between oneself and what is not oneself'[5].

This is only tentatively sketched as an interesting model, and there is one feature of it which I do not understand. It is plain, as Kant has shown us, that without some contrasts and discrimination such as Strawson envisages, we could not identify things in a world of sounds and have a coherent world. But this does not show why there might still not *be* various sounds without a pattern which makes discrimination possible. A mere flow of sound would still not be a universal. What occurs, occurs as it does; likewise for thoughts. There is, indeed, a problem as to what a thought could *be* wholly detached from other thoughts. But a thought is in the first place a mental state. We may also use the same term, as we use 'idea', for the content of a mental state which more than one person might entertain. It is in this sense that we share our thoughts. But, as a mental state, a thought is not any kind of concept or universal. It is an event; and, however hard it may be, in some situations, to have a convenient way to identify certain events, they do not, for that reason, become universals.

It is, indeed, hard to see why, in a world of sounds alone, there might not be many hearings of precisely the same sort of sound at the same time. We could hardly say that they were heard at different places, but there could be different hearings. One is led at once to ask, however, *who* could be hearing them. And the major difficulty, for Strawson, I suspect, is that, for other reasons, he is not able to allow for a subject who could hear the sounds in the conditions now envisaged. In the absence of any way of placing the sounds, and also of their being heard by this person rather than that, one is apt to drift into the supposition that, if there could be such a sound at all, it could not be a particular instantiation of anything and must thus be some kind of universal or type. That is, however, quite mistaken. For if we allow of sounds which are not contrasted and identified in fact, and without a distinct subject hearing them, they still must be thought to be occurrences which could, in fact, be duplicated at the same time. Likewise for thoughts, as mental occurrences. But what all this points to, in the last resort, is the web of unnecessary difficulties which we weave for ourselves when we try to think of any kind of mental occurrence without some kind of subject. But this brings us to what will be for many the more substantial difficulty raised by the idea of a world of totally disembodied existence, namely that also put by Strawson in his discussion of monads when he asks 'why there might not be an indefinite number of indistinguishable monad-particulars of a given monad-type'[6]. In other words, to put the question as it arises for us in our discussion – how are persons identified in a world of thoughts alone? We may suppose that the thoughts themselves are made possible by having had some of them in our previous embodied existence, or we may leave it as an ultimate mystery in the same way as we must in the last resort leave the existence of any kind of world. But we must ask what would make it a *world*, and not just a stream of events; and this is bound up with the question of our own identity as apprehending subjects.

Putting it very simply, how, in a totally disembodied state, would anyone know who he was, or who anyone else was? How would communication be possible? For anyone who holds that a corporeal factor is essential for all identification of persons, as is the case for Strawson and most other English-speaking philosophers today, the answer is plain, namely that there could be no answer to such questions. If we do not take that line, the question is open, but it will seem to many an exceptionally difficult one. At one level, however, it presents no particular difficulty if the main theme of this book is sound. For, if I am right, every creature will be the creature he is and aware of being the being that he is, in a basic though not reflective sense, in the fact of having experience of any kind. This will hold in another world as much as in this one – indeed in any world, for it is inescapable, it seems to me, in having any kind of experience at all, whether extremely elementary or marvellously rich.

But would we know that we were the persons who had lived before on this earth? Not inevitably. We saw earlier that it was conceivable that persons should be reincarnated and live again in this world. In many such cases there would, presumably, be no recollection of the previous life. Similarly, it could happen that we should come to exist in another world with no recollection of the present one. As hinted earlier, we must presume some limits to the changes we may undergo, especially in the first stage of any such existence. But there is no inconsistency in our *being* the persons we now are in another existence even though we had in one existence no awareness of the other. We would not, of course, *ex hypothesi, know* that we were the beings we had been before. But suppose we abandon this hypothesis. Could we know more? Could we know anything of our previous life?

Presumably we could. For we might remember it. But here again we come up against the stock questions about memory. How could a memory be checked in a wholly disembodied state? The first point to make in answer, here as earlier, is that memory seems to be largely self-authenticating. When I wake up in the morning and begin to remember where I am and what I did yesterday, even before I open my eyes, I firmly trust my memory as such, notwithstanding that it has let me down on occasion. Likewise, if I found myself in another world, with my present kind of body or with none, I might still have a very clear recollection of the kind of things I would normally remember now about my own life and events in this world. If I can exist or come to be in a state of thoughts alone, there seems to be no reason why these thoughts should not include my recollections of the kind of life I had departed. Indeed, I might not at once be aware that I was in another world. I might just continue, as I might before I stir and open my eyes on awaking, deep in some train of thought or reverie; and this would include recollections of what had happened before, perhaps very vivid ones. If my death had come about suddenly, perhaps by instant heart failure at night, I might not at once be aware that I had died. I might then continue much as I would on awaking now before I begin to take stock of my environment. My recollections could then be substantially the same in the one case as in the other. True, there is no brain to 'store' my memories. But that would apply in a world of imaged bodies as well, and if we are to entertain the idea of life in another world at all, we are *ipso facto* dispensing with the present dependence of our mental life on our brains. If we have memories in another world of images, there appears to be no reason, in principle, why we should not have them in a world of thoughts alone.

Admittedly, the images I might have in a next world of images could help out my memories a lot, just as I remember my flight to New York as soon as I wake up in a New York hotel. But this does not seem to be essential. Nor is it clear that, if we think of the next world as one in which there are no images presented to us in a coherent and systematic way such as would provide a world or environment in which we can function, we have yet to debar from a more exclusively mental world such images as we might have in our own reveries. The latter would seem to be a reasonable stage between a proper world of images and a world of just thoughts alone. Indeed, having lived in a physical world and with images of physical reality, it is hard to see how we could exclude this altogether from our private cogitations. But our memories themselves are not images, and with or without such severely private images, there appears to be no reason in principle why we should not have memories in the next world of life in the present one, nor why we should not take them to be genuine and trust them.

The coherence of our memories might also be invoked to give them additional credibility. The possibility could be raised, of course, that it was a coherent fabrication of some kind, a dream. But dreams are not usually as coherent as that; and if one found oneself in another world, whatever its nature, with firm recollections, as they seemed, of the substance of what we normally know and retain of our life in this world, the presumption would surely be, most of all if our 'recollections' had the feel of what our memories are normally like, that they were genuine and could be trusted.

If, in addition, it is thought that we had, in our totally disembodied state, as in a quasi-embodied one, some means of knowing about life as it is on earth, and I do not see why this should be ruled out by the difficulty of our knowing now what form it could take, then there would be ways in which we could check and confirm our memories of our previous existence – we could check what we remembered against what we otherwise found to be the case. Moreover, we might, with or without contact with the world left behind, check our memories against the memories of other departed spirits if communication with them is possible. I shall return to the last point shortly. But assuming that there is communication, the fact that our own memories tallied with the memories of others would surely help to confirm our confidence in them. We would have to be under some very great delusion indeed for our memories to overlap and coincide in a coherent way without their being properly memories of a previous existence at all. In the absence of any reason to suspect some colossal deceit that is practiced on us all, if we exorcise the Demon again – and why should we not? – the natural thing to conclude would surely be that our seeming memories of a former life were genuine ones.

In addition we might find in the patterns of our thoughts, as was hinted earlier we might in the images presented to us, some clue as to what was going on in this earth or some way in which the present world might dependably reflect itself in our thoughts in the next. The case is indeed harder than when we are dealing with images which have a firmer existence, over against us as it might be put, than thoughts which are just states of our minds. But thoughts could come with a significant insistence and that again be varied according to the way we adjust the direction of our attention in response. But this itself takes us into the general question of communication and apprehension of anything other than our own states of mind in a world of thoughts alone. This, I imagine, will be the crucial question for those who can be induced to consider the present possibility. If the question of communication can be dealt with at all, there should be no insuperable problem about some kind of contact with the world left behind as well.

Let us ask then how, in a world without impressions or images, or at least without images that presented us with a fairly stable and coherent environment in distinction from merely private reverie, we might ever get out of the privacy of our own thoughts and have intercourse with other beings. Is not solipsism a peculiarly menacing spectre when we think along the present lines? It certainly is, but I do not think we should be wholly daunted.

The first thought that occurs to us when we consider possible communication in a totally disembodied state is that of telepathy. We may think of telepathy as just a strange thing that happens, as confirmed by the evidence, without being able to say anything in further explanation. Some people, we would then say, do just receive these communications, or in the case of clairvoyance become aware of certain things, without our being able to say anything further in explanation of how it comes about. But, in fact, we are able in some cases to say more. A picture flashes into the mind or some kind of voice is heard. If, however, we take these accompaniments to be incidental and not strictly part of the mode of communication, then, in what we may thus

call 'neat' telepathy, we have something which could operate just as well in a world of thoughts as in any other. It just
happens that minds are able to communicate in this direct
way – and at the same time to identify the source of the
communication. But it is not impossible to go a good deal
further in explanation of how the communication takes
place, and how disembodied spirits might identify one
another.

Suppose a spirit, in a totally disembodied state, were
deep in some particular train of thought. He suddenly finds
himself distracted by the eruption of a very different
thought which yet has some relevance to what he is thinking; he is pulled suddenly away on to another track. Now
this is not altogether unusual for any of us. Our thoughts
wander, concentration is broken without any obvious external cause. We have sudden brain-waves and hit on some
novel idea to try out. There is no reason to suppose that
anyone has sent us this. It 'came out of the blue'. But suppose that, as we turn our attention to the new hunch, the
same thing happens again and that our own deliberate
directing of our attention along a particular course is syste-
matically broken at certain points to direct us more and
more effectively to our target. Then we might begin to feel
that we were being cunningly helped by someone able to
influence our thoughts in this way. Helpful distractions
might not be the only ones. Angry feelings might well
up within us at some turn our thoughts may be taking,
or an unexpectedly strong burst of gladness. We might
have an unexpected feeling of foreboding at another
stage. These could be odd turns of our own thought; it
may be our sub-consciousness that is helping us along.
Perhaps this is how one's mind works. But if in the process, we find ourselves confronted with quite unexpected
novelties, if we find ourselves somewhat insistently
drawn away at crucial points from the course our
thoughts would otherwise follow, then the impression
would be deepened that some suggestions were being
imported into our thoughts from a source other than
some unsuspected depths of our own minds. The inference might not be conclusive but it could accumulate

strength in the subtleties and variations of the phenomena involved.

It is not irrelevant here to recall that the idea of revelation
has often been understood in the sense of something 'suggested' to the recipient of it. Richard Bell comments in
these terms on the use of the Arabic word awhā.[1]. Tradition
claims, in Islamic religion, that the message of God was
brought to Muhammad by the angel Gabriel. But there are
only two references to Gabriel in the Qur'an and they do not
concern the most inspired parts. Nor is there any hint that
the angel appeared in visible form. The commonest account
is that Allah or his messenger *suggests* something. The word
awhā has come to be used for revelations given to
Muhammad but originally, as is reflected in the Qur'an
itself, it stood for something flashing into one's mind in a
moment of inspiration. Perhaps it was in these terms more
than in the course of some actual apparition that Luther
argued with the devil, or that other saints, in the stress of
temptation, felt that something was whispered to them or
that someone was telling them this or that. This does not
mean that the inference to an evil presence was straightway
justified, but it does show how strongly it may sometimes
be felt that what is welling up in our own thoughts is alien
to our own mind and seems to be suggested to us from
without. Revelation has certainly been taken seriously in
such terms.

Responses in the way of further emotional reactions
could also play a prominent part in the process as a whole.
We may feel elated at what has come about and glow with
some kind of incipient gratitude, only to find ourselves suf-
fused at once with a deprecatory feeling. Once the initial
stages are over and we begin firmly to distinguish fairly
sharply between the natural course of our own thoughts
and what appears to be suggested from without, the process
can be put to further, more deliberate test. We may firmly
direct our thoughts in a certain way, or dwell on certain
ideas of gratitude or request and then find our thoughts
again shaping themselves, unexpectedly but appropriately,
in a specific direction. The influence so detected need not,
however, always have the same character, and on the basis

of varying but sustained patterns of influence, we may be able to identify a number of distinct agencies that affect us and respond to the way we set our own thoughts in turn. Once agencies of this kind are presumed to be detected, we may concentrate on occasion on one or other of them and find the seeming response to be in character. If this is sustained in the case of a number of agencies, this would add considerably to the force of the original presumption; and, as the ramifications extend through a wealth of concomitant variations, there might be very strong grounds for supposing that we are in communication in these ways with other spirits.

Nor need we stay at the level of isolated contact with each agent in a circumscribed context of his own. We might convey what X has intimated to us to Y and, on the basis of his reaction, to Z before coming back to our original contact, all of which might be accompanied and affected by emotional reactions at various stages. Nor need it be thought that all the communications have the same level of richness. Some may even be hostile, and we learn to be on our guard against them, although some religious traditions, but by no means all, set the 'redeemed' for good beyond all hostile influence in the next life. But what matters at the moment is that once identification becomes possible in principle there is no obvious hindrance to ramification into all manner of social relations and diversities of character.

The process by which such relations are sustained may, however, seem very cumbersome and artificial; it depends upon very deliberate manipulation of the course of our own thoughts and attentiveness. But that may only seem so to us in our attempts to reconstruct what the operation itself is like. Analysis of our present communications through apprehension of the world as it presents itself to our perceptions might also leave the same impression. Communication is a very complicated business, and reflection upon it may seem to take us far away from the smooth and easy reality. That is why some philosophers, most of all today, become rather impatient with such analyses. They tell us that we see tables and chairs and listen to people, which seems a far cry from elaborate moves with what is presented in visual fields, etc. But that is the nature of analysis. It does not in any way belie the spontaneity and ease of the process so analysed itself. Nor is such analysis suspect for that reason. A proper account of perception may be very complicated, but that does not mean that it is bound to be faulty, or that our perception of the world of nature may not be simple and easy.

We have also to remember, in a context like the present one, that we are trying to construct a possible mode of communication, in very exceptional conditions, from within our own very different experience of communication through an independently identifiable order of nature. What seems bewildering to us, accustomed to our present conditions, may not be so to creatures whose regular milieu is altogether different. This may also make a process which seems laboured or cumbersome to us smooth and spontaneous within the process.

Perhaps we could also view our tentative reconstruction along similar lines to Professor Strawson when he thinks of his merely auditory world, not as something which he considers strictly possible, but as a model which may help to bring out features of the conceptual structure adequate to the world as, in fact, we actually find it. There may be a good deal more to total disembodied exsistence than we can envisage when impelled to think of it by simply eliminating bodily or quasi-bodily features and being left with nothing within the compass of our understanding but thoughts alone. The structure of our world of thoughts alone may be related to further features of a mode of being of which we have no conception beyond the clue to be found in the structure of a world of thoughts alone.

The same consideration may be very relevant also when we consider a further criticism or reaction to which many will be much disposed, and very understandably, when they think of a world where solipsism is only avoided by patterns and manipulations of attention within what is otherwise our private communing. For even if every reliance be placed upon seeming communications from identifiable sources, the world and community within which this happens will seem an extremely dull or anaemic one; not altogether removed from the unearthly ballet of bloodless categories. Give me, someone may say, a world of tangible realities, of colours and sounds, of warm flesh and blood, not the rarefied world of purely mental exchanges. This reaction may well underestimate what may, in fact, be achieved, in vividness and liveliness of mutual contact and in closeness of personal involvement in exchanges of a strictly intellectual kind and in the co-operative pursuit of intellectual rigour. Intellectual friendship is not to be despised. But there may, in addition, when all that the word 'bodily' conveys or suggests is abandoned, be some other compensating features of existence of which we have no conception at all, other dimensions of being which guarantee their own closeness and richness of personal relations and which may enhance immensely in other ways the richness of our experience as a whole.

This is, in fact, the expectation of many who look forward to a future existence. They anticipate that not only will the ills and privations of the present life be removed, but also that we shall, in some cases at once and in others after passing through various stages, enter into a much more glorious state of which we have no conception now. This also means, as I shall stress again, that we must not be unduly daunted by difficulties which present themselves in our attempts to work out a consistent and plausible notion of what it must be like to survive our death. There is bound to be much that is obscure to us now about such a possibility. It has not been 'disclosed to us what we shall be' and we must be content to 'see in a glass darkly'. But one feature of the expectation that we shall enter on some richer and more glorious state of being is that, in this new condition, the glory of God will be reflected more brightly. We shall find ourselves closer to God and more sure of his presence. For some this will not matter so much as the assurance they already have of the character of God and his will for us. Christians, for example, do not think that anything will ever surpass the assurance of God's concern in what he has done for us in Christ. This is, for them, the supreme act of God towards us and nothing can eclipse it. There can be nothing finer than having this assurance and the sweetness of the relationship which it makes possible. But it could also be maintained that this supreme and final work of redeeming love can itself be seen yet more splendidly in some richer and riper mode of being with finer endowments. It is, in any case, the greater glory of God that comes first.

The last expectation is carried by some to the point of our being taken up wholly into the being of God. What does our trivial existence matter? God is all in all, and we shall one day shed the anxiety and frustration of a limited finite existence and lose ourselves wholly in God. There is precedent in many religions for this expectation. We are restless, it is said, till we find ourselves in God; it is in him alone that we find fulfilment of ourselves. St Paul declares that his life is hidden with Christ in God. He glories in nothing but the Cross of Christ. Many mystics have spoken in the same vein of being lost in the life of God. But we have also to tread warily here. For there are many ways in which this absorption into the life of God may be understood. For some it is plainly metaphor. Others take it at its face value and assume that the secret of the blessedness to which we may look forward is that of a total elimination of our independent finite existence through its absorption into the being of God. This is what is held by many mystics, especially in Eastern religions. That brings us to a vast topic which has to be considered properly on its merits and needs a book to itself. Some comment is essential, however, on the idea that the life eternal is, in fact, a life of total absorption into the being of God. That will be attempted next.

10 Mysticism and Monism

The idea that in any destiny we may have, beyond our present existence, there is no need to preserve our personal identity, or the sense of identity that we now have, has always had a strong appeal. It is deeply embedded in many Eastern cultures and religions, and in related metaphysical systems. Strong support for it may also be found from time to time in the West. There are two main forms of this idea to be noted. The first is the view that, although the ultimate distinctness of persons must be surrendered, there is still an important, indeed indispensable, part to be played by the individual as a mode or element of some kind in the one whole of being to which he belongs. This is the view which appears to be most common in Hinduism, although this is an area where it is not easy to generalise. Western thought, when it becomes explicit, usually favours this qualified form of monism more than any other, though the affirmations of some Western mystics appear, if taken neat, to go much further towards the total elimination of the finite self.

The attractions, as well as the difficulties, of this kind of monism may be seen to good advantage in certain metaphysical systems. In the teaching of Plotinus, for example, we have the somewhat novel but difficult idea of emanation. Individual souls are emanations from the One, via *nous* or intelligence which, like *logos*, in some of the later Greek forms of this idea, stands somewhere between the transcendent One and other particular beings. A major difficulty for this view is to account for spontaneity and for accountability and evil. Association with matter was sometimes thought to provide the key to the latter problem, and, on occasion, matter tended to be regarded in this way as some independent reality opposed to, or at least limiting, the One. On the whole, Plotinus resisted this drift into metaphysical dualism and was inclined to regard all things as ultimately good when viewed properly in their place in a harmonious whole. There are questions also about the purpose of our existence in its present embodied form, sometimes regarded, as in parts of Plato's teaching, as a falling away into association with inferior being, though Plotinus does not, any more than Plato, think of the body as inherently degrading. It is plain, however, that whatever accounts for the initial emanation and the existence of the world of nature as we normally find it, the aim should be to draw away from the limited existence we have now into a more ideal mode of being and eventually return to the One from whence we came, thus, in famous words, completing 'the flight of the alone to the Alone'.

There are many problems in this kind of monistic philosophy, and Plotinus was not unaware of them. It is interesting to follow his many sincere attempts to cope with his difficulties. This is not the place to try that. The main point for us is the diminishing value of the kind of existence and activity we have now. It did not lead for Plotinus, as it did with some, to a low regard for all the good we can do in this life or to stagnation and apathy. For he held, again very like Plato, that it was by discipline and by proper moral and intellectual endeavour that we draw away from the ills and limitations of our present existence and achieve the purification which fits us for higher things. All the same, the relations we have in this world and the interest we may take in the daily round of it, tend to become trivial and to have no place in the destiny we eventually achieve. They may present obstacles to be overcome at present, but in themselves they have no abiding place. This is well reflected in a feature of Plotinus' teaching which has an interesting bearing on some matters we were discussing earlier. He holds, in a way that is not unlike some forms of theosophy today, that there are two sorts of bodies, celestial and terrestrial; and he also speaks sometimes of a double soul. Related to this is the notion of two kinds of memory – or two 'faculties' of memory as some would put it. When a man is dead, the higher soul no longer remembers any of the things that happened to it while in the body; the lower soul still remembers. We are also, all of us, one with intelligence or the one Soul, and eventually with the One from which all emanate. As individualisations of Soul all souls communicate by extra-sensory means, which anticipates some of the suggestions which H. H. Price has made from time to time. Whether this is properly thought of as communication is a difficult problem, and much would turn here on how the souls are thought to be many and also one. No memory is allowed to Intelligence and Soul.

Intriguing possibilities are raised by all these suggestions, and some of them might be put to interesting use in contexts other than the monistic metaphysics of Plotinus himself. The student who wishes to pursue the topics of this book further could do worse than undertake a close look at the works of Plotinus and some of the Gnostics against whom he argued. But the point that emerges most clearly for us is that, in fulfilling our proper destiny, we leave behind the cares and concerns which matter most in this life we have now. Home, friends, families, children, the sounds and sights of the multifarious world of nature, all these fade and seem to contribute in no way to the life that supersedes them. What their rationale is, is not plain, and we are bound to wonder why there need ever be 'a flight from the alone to the Alone'. Such problems are not altogether peculiar to monism. They have their counterpart in the idea of Creation and in any consideration of a transcendent or infinite reality. But, in non-monistic views, there is at least the easement of a firm recognition of present reality and of some function it may continue to have in some scheme of things for our eventual destiny. It is not as if life as we know it now had never been.

Plotinus himself has some impressive accounts of the ecstatic states in which the soul finds itself ascending again to its original source, though, for obvious reasons, he can only speak here in 'slantwise' terms, as Evelyn Underhill put it, or metaphorically. Nor does he ever go the whole length of totally repudiating limited or finite existence. It is to take care of the latter that we have the notable doctrine of emanation or, as it has sometimes been called, 'dynamic pantheism'. This is why we keep Plotinus, not always very happily, in the class of what I have called qualified monism. The finite does not altogether disappear, and much that is said about it anticipates what writers of recent times have said about process and development. Plotinus holds, perhaps, a half-way house between qualified monism and the more daring surrender of the many to the One. In any case, there remains for him, as for many others, the problem of finding some proper place in the scheme of things for the variety, warmth and intimacy which conditions so much that we rate most highly at present.

A different form of monism, and one that appears at least to guarantee the place and reality of finite beings more effectively, is that of Spinoza. On his view, a finite thing is a 'mode' of an attribute of the one substance which is God. God exists by necessity and his essence is found in his attributes. These are infinite in number, but every mode is expressed in all the attributes. We only know the attributes of thought and extension, though why this should be is not clear. Our bodies are modes of God in the attribute of extension, and they have their counterpart when the same mode is expressed in our consciousness in the attribute of thought, thus anticipating and providing much of the ancestry of the double aspect version of the identity thesis in accounts of mind and body today. This raises many problems about our own initiative and the autonomy of our thinking. Spinoza tried to cope with these in terms of the adequacy of our ideas. The sting is taken out of what seems to be strict determinism by directing attention to the greater excellence and freedom of the behaviour, which is accompanied by adequate ideas through which we understand better why things occur as they do and identify ourselves with the hand that shapes us. There is also a *conatus* of the modes by which they strive to maintain their place in the several attributes, thus bringing the doctrine as a whole into closer accord with common experience. Immortality is understood mainly in terms of adequate ideas. It is not just that we are immortal in the sense that every mode has to be what it is as an expression of the eternal being of God, but that the more we rise to understanding of this and to an eventual intuitive apprehension of God, the more completely are we taken up into the love of God which is also God's infinite love of himself. There is here no question of duration or of existence in some way beyond the demise of the body, but there is the greatest bliss for us in our intellectual love of God to which we come by the adequacy of our ideas.

On this view, the notion of a personal survival after death is an illusion, but the idea of one's body exists in an eternal way in the mind of God, and the mind one has as a counterpart of this or in the attribute of thought is united with God in the measure that it understands and conceives things under the form of eternity. Spinoza is thus able to declare that 'the human mind cannot be absolutely destroyed with the body, but something of it, which is eternal, remains'[1]. This is, however, a difficult statement, in the context of Spinoza's thought, and there has been much discussion as to what precisely it meant. It is clearly a far cry from survival in the way this would normally be understood. The individual is not preserved in his distinctness, for all that is itself an illusion.

A form of monism which seeks to do greater justice to the way we normally think of ourselves as finite beings is that of Hegel and post-Hegelian idealism. The latter dominated much of both Western and Eastern philosophy at the turn of the century. It also regarded reality as one whole in which everything had its place prescribed by the nature of the whole. This does not mean that our individual existence and our lives in this world are wholly unreal, but they are only real in virtue of their place in the whole. There is no ultimate distinctness, and the impression we may have of a distinct existence is an appearance and an illusion. Indeed, in a sense, all our experience, and the world as we apprehend it, must be thought to be appearance, for the true nature and full reality of everything can only be found when its place in the system as a whole is fully displayed. But nothing is mere appearance or a complete delusion. The more we understand anything, the more we grasp its true reality. The only fully true reality is the one being, the absolute.

The main form of this kind of idealism comes fairly directly from the attempt of Hegel to reduce the gap in Kantian philosophy between the world as organised in our experience and the world as it really is, between phenomenal and noumenal reality in technical terms. There are suggestions in some of Kant's own work that the 'thing in itself' is a completion of the world of which *we* can only have an imperfect apprehension. The objects of our experience are conditioned by or relative to the way we apprehend things, but instead of a sharp dichotomy between such a world and some completely different true reality 'in itself', we have the suggestion that the 'ultimate reality' is the completion or fulfilment of our present experience. A distinctive feature of present experience is the unification of it made possible by the presentation of objects to an abiding subject, as mentioned in another context earlier. When we think of the subject as a focus or centre and no more, the extension and completer unification of our own experience coincides with the similar extension of the experience of others, so that eventually there is only one completed whole in which the place of everything is settled by the nature of the whole to which it belongs – the peep-holes are enlarged, as we saw earlier, until there is only the one vista.

The difficulties in this position are those which confront all forms of monism, namely those of accounting for our apparent consciousness of our own distinctness and the sense we have in consequence of our freedom and accountability. Indeed, it is difficult to find a proper place for evil of any kind in a monistic idealist system. There can only be seeming evil from our limited point of view, and this is hard to accept when we think of distressing forms of suffering or vile forms of moral turpitude. The defenders of this kind of idealism tried to cope with the difficulties in various ways which can not be properly surveyed here, some stressing in particular the importance of finite centres of unification within the reality of the whole, and some making drastic modifications in the principles of an idealist metaphysics. They could certainly allow for our present lives having a significance beyond their own temporal span, and it is not out of place for a very rigorous idealist like Bernard Bosanquet to write, in a celebrated (but, alas, now somewhat neglected) chapter of his *Value and Destiny of the Individual* of life as 'a vale of soul-making', in Keats' famous phrase. In some sense life is conserved in this form of idealism, but it can only be in as much as our present attainments are taken up into the total corpus of experience in the one whole of being, giving, as Pringle-Pattison put it 'some peculiar flavour or tang to a universal experience'[2]. It is not easy to see how Pringle-Pattison himself, despite his protest and insistence on the place of the finite individual as an indispensable finite centre of experience, can avoid the ultimate merging of the individual in the life of the whole. It is not surprising that he takes refuge in the ambiguities of the claim that 'religious truth is in its essence practical' and that 'the idea of immortality has no religious significance . . . if we separate it from the idea of eternal life as a realised possession'. The fate of the individual, as we normally think of him, becomes very uncertain on these views.

There is, however, one position which is much more extreme than the ones indicated hitherto – and much more difficult to expound. For there are some who seem to maintain that it is a mistake to try to give any account of what we normally take to be finite existences. It is an illusion, so it is held, to suppose that there are finite things at all, and especially that there is any kind of self. This is, indeed, a strange view, for we seem to be confronted all the time with the many-hued contents of our present experience, whatever their status. It seems impossible, indeed preposterous, to go back on this. Nothing which presents itself in this way can be a *total* illusion. It must be real in some way, as are our own mental states. The ancestry of the present view is, however, a notable one, beginning in Western thought with Parmenides. He held that there were *a priori* reasons for denying all multiplicity. The nature of thought itself forbids it. Thought involves contrast, and contrast negation, affirming what is not. But this last is what we cannot do, for how can we think what is not real? There are flaws in this, as Plato and others were quick to point out. The unreal in negation is not wholly unreal. But the lure of a position like that of Parmenides persisted, although many who held it seem to have faltered sooner or later. Many mystics have claimed that, in mystical experience, all variation and all multiplicity dissolves and is seen to be illusion. There is only the One. For those who have not had such an experience, it is very difficult to know what is being claimed, at least if the claim is advanced in its more outright form. Some mystics interpret their experience more in terms of the views noted earlier in this chapter. But others defy the obvious difficulties in going all the way with Parmenides.

One such thinker in our own day is the late Professor W. T. Stace. He would not, however, defend a wholly unqualified monism. Indeed, he says at one point that such a position is a 'silly' one. But he is prepared all the same to affirm, in the most literal sense, that there is only the One. 'The many' is illusion. But how can there be this illusion? The answer is to rest in downright unqualified paradox. There is only the One, there are also the many, and we must not blunt the outright contradictory character of such a stance, or take what is said to be metaphorical or allusive. Contradiction is the answer, total and not provisional, and it seems that we must not be daunted by having to accept contradiction in this way. Stace defends his position at many points, and I have tried elsewhere to deal with his arguments. The main point I made was that Stace has not quite understood what we are to make of the idea of transcendence. In finding the world and ourselves to be essentially dependent, that is to require to be sustained in being by some reality complete and self-sustaining as no finite being can be, we posit a reality altogether different from ourselves of whose nature we can form no proper conception – it is beyond, eternal, uncreated. We cannot know what it must be like to be such a reality, and that is a position with problems of its own which cannot be examined here. But if we are right in thinking that the essence of God is thus, in principle, incapable of being known by us, it is also wrong to try to explain how the required dependence must be understood or how the finite is related to infinite being. But if we try to make sense of what is bound to elude our understanding in this way, to 'scale down' the transcendent 'to the logical plane of the intellect' in Stace's own words, we are certain to end up in irreducible paradox and contradiction. We know God obliquely, not in his essence, though that is no bar to knowing him intimately and closely. But if we try to give an exhaustively rational account of him, or of our relation to him, we shall find ourselves committed to various forms of unreason, including the curious questioning of the reality of finite things. Our lives are rooted in mystery, but we must recognise this without presuming to fathom it further for ourselves. Creation will not then have to look like absorption into the source of our being. We can remain, in all our dependence, distinct existences.

A further feature of Stace's position is of special interest to us. He draws a fairly sharp distinction between two sorts of mysticism. The first is extrovert mysticism. The peculiarity of this is that the mystic takes his start from the common experience of a variety of objects in the world around us. He finds these dissolving into a unity in which their diversity is lost or seen to be unreal. But there is needed an awareness of 'the many' for a start, and, in some cases, the mystic never quite manages to leave 'the many' behind. This is not the most perfect form of mysticism, as concessions are made to the impression we have of variety and change. In a more final and proper form of mysticism, namely introvert mysticism, we turn away from the changing world of variety around us and concern ourselves solely with our own inner being, with the self as essentially self or subject. The self as subject is not capable of being described or characterised. It is not an object to be given its place and mark among others. It is not part of the world but over against the world. For this reason there is nothing to distinguish one such 'pure self' from another. There are no barriers or boundaries; a confluence seems inevitable. Every self is one with every other and with the supreme or infinite self at the heart of the universe. There is, in fact, nothing but the One Supreme Self. In realising this the mystic attains his goal in a blessed state of complete union with the One.

In following this argument it is not easy to avoid the feeling that the world of the many is being rather unfairly dropped out of account. It is hard to deny it by just averting our eyes and directing attention elsewhere. But there is a point of much greater importance for us. I agree readily with Professor Stace, as should be quite evident by now, that we cannot describe or characterise the self in the most basic sense of our selfhood. But the true import of holding this seems to me, all the same, quite the reverse of the way Stace understands it. For, on my view, the way the self is indescribable and incapable of being identified is bound up with an essential distinctness and irreducibility of it. We know our own being in being the creatures we are and no other, and for this reason, as I have stressed at more length elsewhere[3], any question of a confluence of selves or a merging of ourselves in the infinite is ruled out. The consideration which seems in one way most favourable to Professor Stace's view cuts, in fact, in precisely the opposite direction.

Closely related to the last point, and very prominent in the history of this subject, is the failure to draw a proper distinction between the very different senses in which the finite self and the infinite respectively do not admit of being characterised. The finite self just cannot be described because of its distinctness and the way this is known. That may be thought of God also, but the infinite is beyond location and description in a quite different way, namely by being infinite and not admitting of any limitation or placing. There are no parts of the being of God, and how God exists in an eternal or uncreated way is beyond even the most incipient comprehension by us, though we see the necessity of his being as the ground of all else. Many, from remote times to the present day, have rung the familiar changes on the sense in which the ultimate is 'beyond being and knowledge', in Plato's famous phrase. We do not know the essence of God, though we may come to know him intimately in other ways. We have no notion what it is like in itself to be God. But this is a peculiarity of the being of God as infinite being. He is, in his essence, beyond the world of description in the ordinary sense. He is not one object among others but transcendent or absolute being. We are also in a very limited way transcendent, since we are not bound to the present. But this is a very different matter. The sense in which the self is private and known initially only to itself has nothing to do with infinity, though there are other analogies, as we have seen, between our knowledge of God and of one another.

If, however, these matters are overlooked and we find ourselves thinking of our own elusiveness in the same terms as the elusiveness of genuine transcendence or infinite being, there may be imported into the awareness we have of our own selfhood something of the quality of the mysterious infinite; and from this two things result. Firstly, it becomes more plausible to suppose that we come to be ourselves identified with God, something of the quality of our awareness of divinity having spilled over into awareness of the self. Secondly, we find the supposed elimination of the self more acceptable when it seems to be a matter of being taken up into something which we seem to be already. The peculiar joy which some contemplatives take in what seems to be the total eclipse of their own existence owes much to the sense which they also have of fulfilling their own true being in the infinite richness of the being of God. Their own distinctness is taken up into the ecstatic awareness of the sublimity of God, and there is thus no feeling of loss but of becoming aware of what, in fact, they are already. This goes a very long way I suspect to explain the paradox of the joy with which the seemingly total elimination of the self is expected in some religious attitudes of mind.

The present point must not be confused with the proper and more easily understandable relief and serenity we may feel at the prospect of the purification of self in the elimination of narrow self-concern and anxiety. The two points are easily conflated, since the attainment of the sense of passing beyond the limitations of finite selfhood is furthered most by the disciplines and conduct which take us away from excessive concern with our own success and prosperity. The kind of selflessness anticipated here is in no way inconsistent with, but on the contrary strongly supports, the sense that, while God is not ourselves but rather our author and sustainer, yet he is also 'all in all'. To be wholly taken up with the glory and the love of God is one thing, we may very understandably and fittingly lose ourselves in him in this sense. But it is another matter to be joyfully lost to ourselves in the sense of finding our own true reality in the removal of finite limitations and ascent to some absolute existence.

It has often been said that there is a close affinity between the repudiation of the self in Buddhist thought or philosophy and the denial of the self by David Hume. There is truth in this, but we must not exaggerate it. Hume was an exceptionally secular urbane thinker. His empiricism precluded his recognising any self which he would not discover by looking into himself. The motivation and intellectual ethos of Buddhism is vastly different. Its main positions are not established in the first instance by close analysis. It is par excellence the religion of contemplation, acute though its thought is also in major regards. It may be in some ways more a philosophy than other religions, but we shall do it scant justice if we think of it as exclusively a system of philosophy. Attainment comes in Buddhism by illumination and enlightenment, and in this proper context we may find that more light is thrown on the aspiration and claims of Buddhism by considerations such as the conflation of the sense of the transcendent, however named, and the sense of the elusiveness of finite selfhood than by the affinities with Western sceptical thought.

In brief illustration of this let me quote a few passages from a recent study, namely *Happiness and Immortality*, by P. J. Saher who presents to us, in this book, the substance of the teaching of a devoted Buddhist scholar, George Grimm. Saher writes:

> That none of the familiar definitions of our 'I' is adequate is due to the fact that here an essential requirement of every definition is overlooked. If it is a question of discovering an object and identifying it as such, then at least *one* unmistakable feature of it must be known.[4]

But it is not possible to find such a feature. 'No Western philosopher has discovered such an *infallible* criterion for our *real* "I" '[5]. There is no way of distinguishing in these terms 'between the objects of cognition and my "I" as the

Self or subject of cognition; if I am not to run the risk of regarding as my Self something that is not it'[6]. This is a theme with which we are now familiar, whether in Kantian philosophy or in contemporary work like that of Professor Shoemaker. The affinity becomes particularly close in the way memory is conceived and the prominence given to it. 'Recollection, however, is not a mere survey of former images or pictures now reappearing, but rather a recognition of them as something experienced by ourselves'[7]. We must 'meditate on this' as a matter of 'insight', of 'immediate certainty' and 'intuitive cognition'.

So far we seem to follow closely the lines of argument favoured in the present book, and those who look closely at the numerous quotations from Buddhist texts with which Saher supports and illustrates his interpretation, will realise how much we have to learn in these matters from the wisdom of the East. But Saher goes on to maintain that because the self cannot be circumscribed and bounded in the same way as an object of experience, it is not itself in time or limited, and he proceeds to speak of the 'true' or 'inner' self in terms that seem appropriate only to infinite or transcendent reality and the inner peace that comes from contemplation of the latter. We are urged to

> withdraw into ourselves, into our real Self that is free from all attributes, into the primary ground of being-in-itself, into *Nirvāṇa*. In this way, we experience deathless, eternal, perfect well-being (*acolam sukham*) just as such bliss was experienced by the Buddha when he withdrew utterly into himself[8].

In the same terms Saher also writes:

> But then *what are we*, if we are neither body nor mind? In the phenomenal world *everything* is made up of mind and body; such a world consists *only* of these *two* elements, although in varying degrees and combinations. Something that is neither body nor mind is beyond the phenomenal world, and can no longer be grasped by cognition, any more than ultra-violet rays can be perceived by our eyes; hence we can no longer picture it to

ourselves. Thus it is for us inconceivable, indescribable, and unfathomable.

Consequently our true self is unimaginable, inconceivable, indescribable and unfathomable, just because it lies beyond our 'body plus mind'.

'A perfect one, freed from 'body plus mind', is as profound, immeasurable, and unfathomable as the great ocean', says the Buddha. Meister Eckhart says: 'The soul (after its salvation) has lost its name in the unity of divine being; therefore it is no longer called soul there, its name is 'immeasurable being'; And again: 'What the soul is in its deepest ground has never yet been discovered'[9].

Yet again we read:

This absolute reality, 'the great point of rest at the centre of the universe' is our eternal destiny. In it, which at the same time is 'the great point of support of the universe', is grounded the miracle of immortality. In it are grounded the marvels of evolution, the numberless worlds that present themselves to us as the starry heavens, in it is grounded *everything*.

'In thy nothing – (the primary ground is not accessible to our cognition) – I hope to find [the essence] of the Universe.' Reality is grounded in this incomprehensible and inconceivable primary state; the state beyond all possible cognition.

Everything positive, everything comprehensible, in particular everything good as well as evil, has arisen first on this side of the phenomenal world.

For the man who has found his way back to this primary ground of being, and thus to *Nirvāṇa*, remains there, as 'the highest goal there is in the created and uncreated'; 'the great peace' – 'eternal imperturbability'. It is the great liberation[10].

It would be interesting to look closely into various Buddhist writings and the scriptures of other religions to see how far the movement of thought we find in these passages is reflected in them. But that would take us far beyond the limits of the present study. I quote these passages here to indicate how easy it is to conflate the elusive nature of the finite self with the mystery of infinite being. This conflation has, in my view, affected the attitude of mind which looks with equanimity, nay with great joy, upon the elimination of our finite existence as such, finding in it a 'return', again in Saher's words, 'to his self beyond the personality'. This is not the only strain in Buddhist thought on these subjects, but it is more extensive than has commonly been assumed, and I incline to the view that it provides the main clue to the acceptance in a religiously exalted frame of mind of much that would otherwise be perplexing if taken seriously, which is not always the case in popular Buddhism.

But while we may find easy adjustment to the prospect of a total eclipse of the self in one sense by thinking of ourselves as wholly at one with eternal or infinite being, this seems to me a radically mistaken notion. Whatever is true of the finite self, it is finite. It is also essentially mental reality. Admittedly one's thoughts and experience could be different, and, if I am correct, this would not affect the basic sense of our identity. On the other hand, our thoughts are not attached to us in an incidental or external way. In an important sense our thoughts and experiences are what we are, they 'belong', as was stressed above, in a very distinctive and irreducible way. One remains the same being when one's mental states change, and would so remain, if I am right, even if these states changed completely or were forgotten, as many of them are in our present life. But, I submit, a self which is not in some mental state is not conceivable, although I would not insist outright that this *must* involve duration. We can form no conception of a timeless state, or indeed of timelessness in any form other than an abstract one, as when we think of universal truth (or, perhaps, all truths) being timeless. But there may be modes of being of which we have no conception now. Nonetheless, a self, whether in time or timeless, which had no content of apprehension of any kind at all, would be far removed from anything we now think of as a self and does not seem to me to be a possible notion. There must be a limit to what we can allow in admitting that there may be features of the universe which are not conceivable by us. Each one knows in his own case what it is to be a self or person, and, I submit, we know ourselves in this way as beings who have essentially some content of our mental state, whether or not that has reference beyond itself. Nor is there any inherent necessity in the existence we find that we have in this way; our entire existence is contingent. We do not, therefore, establish our existence in an immortal and eternal way by simply noting our independence of the most obviously mortal part of us or the part whose destruction seems most effectively to end the kind of existence we enjoy as embodied beings in this world.

My own firm impression therefore remains, namely that, if we continue to exist in some form beyond our earthly span, that must still be some kind of finite existence. A 'future' life may have splendours not known to us now, and it may involve a profounder and more irresistible sense of the presence of God. We may be taken up in a sanctified state into some peculiarly intimate union with God, God may become 'all in all' for us and the centre of all we apprehend, but we could not become God without ceasing to be the contingent creatures we find ourselves to be and forfeiting entirely the identity which would give point to the expectation of some further destiny for *us*. It is, indeed, presumptuous to suppose that we can become God or that God requires us as part of his being. A more plausible view maintains that we were freely created by God, and, while this has its difficulties, they are not as insuperable as the supposition that our existence can be converted into the quality of absolute uncreated being. If we survive we still survive as limited contingent beings. That seems to follow from the kind of beings we find ourselves to be.

11 The Hope of Glory

(It seems evident to me that, if we are to be maintained in being after the present life is ended, there must be continuity of some kind between the life we lead now and our life 'hereafter'. For otherwise there seems to be little point in our having a further existence. It was maintained earlier that we would be the persons we are now in another life even if we had no awareness of our previous existence, and if there were no other form of continuity. This needs to be made clear to bring out properly the nature of the self. On the other hand, it would be odd to have conferred upon us, or in some way to attain to, a further existence (or a series of them) altogether divorced from our existence now. Why not create new beings for whatever purpose is to be served? One form of continuity would be that by which our lives at present affect or determine a future life without our knowing this ourselves or recalling the earlier life. This holds on many forms of the doctrine of Karma. It seems to me, however, that, short of fulfilling some universal requirement of justice in the way implied in that doctrine, there is little to be said for our being maintained in existence with no continuity known to ourselves between one life and another. Admittedly, one life could have some effect on our dispositional set-up in another life without our being aware of how this had come about. But it is hard to see why the same result could not be achieved in some other way, by new creations for example. The great likelihood, it seems then, is that, if we survive our present existence, it will be with some awareness, including, I should add, remembrance, of our life here and now. This is the expectation that most people have if they hope for some future life for themselves. It seems to me that they are fully justified in thinking of it in those terms and that, if it matters for them, it is most likely to do so in the form indicated. This is much enhanced if the hope in question includes, as it usually does, the expectation of a renewal of our fellowship with those whose love and friendship we esteem most now, those who are 'lost awhile' but with whom we hope to be reunited 'some day'.

On the other hand, there is much about a future existence which is bound to remain obscure to us. We speculate cautiously and, in some respects, at our peril. For in our present ignorance we may draw much too crude a picture of the actual reality, and so discourage ourselves and others. At the same time there is much to be said, subject to reasonable caution, for being as realistic as we can if the hope we cherish is to have proper significance. Professor Price at one point appears to go much further. He declares that, if we are thinking of *evidence* for survival, 'there cannot be evidence for something which is completely unintelligible to us'[1]. He also notes that many are put off 'because they find the very conception of Survival unintelligible'[2]. In one sense this is true. No one can expect or believe anything without having *some* idea of what it is that he expects. But it does not follow that we must always have close precision. There is, indeed, one idea which many entertain with very little notion of what it fully involves, namely the idea of God. We have no notion of what it is like to be God, as has been stressed already in this book. But we can still have some idea of infinite and necessary being as involved in the limited being that we have, and obliquely we claim to know more about him. At no point do we claim to fathom his mystery. The idea of God is, of course, a very special one. But it would also be possible to believe in a life in some sense beyond the present one without any clear understanding of what it must be like. We must not carry this too far. If the belief is a belief in personal survival we must pay heed to what we consider essential to our being persons. There must, in the broadest sense, be some content of a mental life which is apprehended by a subject which is distinctively himself and no other. I think we should also insist, if not as a strict requirement of intelligibility, as a certain actual condition, on some fellowship with other similar beings. But we may not find it possible to go further.

We are to be 'changed', the Christian Scriptures say, and 'it doth not yet appear what we shall be'. On this basis some think it mistaken, perhaps improper, to try to go further. I do not share that view; I believe it is very helpful, as Price very clearly thinks, to anticipate cautiously what it would be like to live again. This can prevent our expectations from being too vague or too remote to have relevance for our lives here and now. But the plausibility of speculations like those of Price or my own is in no way essential for a belief in a life hereafter. Many will be content to stay with the reasons they may have for believing that this life is not all without seeking to probe further into the nature of the further life they expect. They are not, in that case, to be put out of court because they can give no further intelligible account, to themselves or others, of what they expect. It is not improper to believe, as many do, in a life after death without any precise understanding of what it may be like. The minimum of intelligibility required is that it should be an existence of the beings we find ourselves in essentials to be. The success or failure of further speculation is not vital, and no one should be put off his faith, if he has reasons for it, by finding attempts to picture a future life unattractive or implausible. He is perfectly entitled to remain piously agnostic about all but the minimal meaningfulness of his hope. The wise course, in my view, is to go cautiously as far as we can in our speculations while avoiding the extremes of a too facile manufacture of another world.

The main point here holds even if, as in Price's case in the context in question, we are mainly concerned with *evidence*. It might be thought that evidence can only be relevant to something of like nature. But this is far from being the case, as may be seen in our knowledge of other minds obtained from observation of the behaviour of their bodies. Even if we think in terms of evidence of the kind which may be provided by psychical research, the conclusions to which we are led may concern a state of being about whose precise nature we may still find ourselves very uncertain. Nor must we forget, as has been stressed already, that there may be much in the universe, even as affecting limited personal existence, of which we have no notion. The most that we require, for a belief in a personal life 'beyond' is that the belief should have sufficient body for it to be a belief in a personal existence. If we fail to go further than that we should not be deterred or dismayed, provided we have adequate reasons for holding to such a belief. But have we in fact, grounds for such a belief? What could they be?

Some philosophers, among them the most notable of all times, have tried to provide philosophical arguments for the immortality of the soul. These are not usually considered to be very successful and they do not often reflect the profundity and incisiveness which gave their authors so prominent a place in the history of the subject. A splendid example is that of Plato. He seems to have had an unwavering belief in the immortality of the soul. He returns to the topic in many of his dialogues, including some which he composed in mid-career, and the *Laws* at the very end, 'Plato's last message to the world' as it has been described. The main theme of his discussion at all points is sharply different from the Christian one in one respect. Although Plato holds that the ultimate key to everything in the universe is the Good, he also thinks of the soul as essentially indestructible. We may make or mar our lot in another life and, indeed, proceed in a sort of rake's progress from one life to another until eventually we reach a stage of no return, a defilement for which there is no redress leaving us in Tartarus like an 'outer darkness' from which we do not emerge. But the soul is not destroyed; defilement does not lead to total disintegration. The reason for this is that the soul just cannot rid itself of its most essential feature in its affinity with eternal truth and the Good. The natural habitat of the soul is the world of forms and this is a world of eternal reality. The soul never forfeits this, however it betrays it, and by the same token it existed before the present life; it partakes of the divine[3] and for that reason it is itself eternal.

This, as we have seen, does not mean for Plato that the soul has the same sort of reality as the forms, and here we reach difficult terrain on which we cannot stay in this book. The soul is not an ordinary particular for Plato, but it is particular and individual in a way that is more like the particular things of the world than the eternal reality of the forms, genuine and objective though that is. Plato never quite resolved the problem of where the soul lies in-between the world of becoming and the world of being and forms. He maintains with some fervour in the 'Sophist'[4] against 'the friends of forms' (but who they are is not altogether clear) that we must have room for 'change, life, soul' and that we cannot have 'intelligence without having life'. Pringle-Pattison is quite right, I believe, in insisting that 'it was a conscious and individual immortality in which Plato believed'[5]. But this was not a conferred immortality, nor was it something to be gained or lost. It was the nature of the soul to be immortal, and this was because it partook in an essential way of the eternal reality of the forms and the Good.

Plato is not altogether consistent in his account of the involvement of the soul with the body, although in saying this we have to remember that most of what he does say on this question is in the form of myth or fable. In the 'Phaedrus' he carries over into the pre-natal state the three-fold division of the soul into reason, spirit and appetite. The latter at least is normally associated with the body, but here we have the slightly different view that it is by yielding to this lower element that the soul (in the figure of the charioteer driving two unequally yoked steeds) loses her feathers and drops to earth to become embodied. In the 'Timaeus' he goes further and suggests that soul and body are everywhere united and that human souls especially are 'implanted in bodies by necessity'. But it seems also plain that the proper home of the soul is not in the world of becoming but in the world of forms, and it is because of this association that it is indestructible. It is in respect of the soul as it is uncontaminated by excesses of our baser nature and intended for its high destiny in the world 'above' – it is of this that Plato speaks so movingly and consistently as the chief concern of man. This is a man's real self and nothing matters so much as a man's 'care for his soul'.

This care involves intellectual discipline of a rigorous kind and also high moral living which includes the selfless service of others; it is not crassly self-centred. The soul is what is truly divine in us and nothing matters so much as that we should nurture and cherish it. In the 'Apology' Socrates declares: 'For I do nothing but go about persuading you all, old and young alike, not to take thought for your persons or your properties, but first and chiefly to care about the greatest improvement of the soul'[6]. In the 'Laws' we read: 'Of all the things which a man has, next to the Gods, his soul is the most divine and most truly his own'[7]. The famous comparison with the sea-god Glaucus, as reproduced earlier[8], may be recalled in the same context.

We have here what Pringle-Pattison has described as a primary or fundamental conviction of Plato. He made it central and he never wavered over it. But beyond expressing his conviction that the soul, in its affinity with abiding truth and supreme goodness, is essentially abiding or eternal, Plato does not take us very far in more explicit and systematic commendation of his view. We remain mostly at the level of primary conviction or the visionary or prophetic utterance which we find in the myths. Where argument is invoked, it has not the impressiveness of the prophetic declaration of faith.

It is hard, for example, to take very seriously the argument we find in the *Phaedo*. Everything, we are told, has an opposite. Sleeping and waking states alternate, and likewise life and death are opposites. Where there is death there must also be life, and the dead must therefore return to life. One could prove all manner of improbable things by this argument. In the 'Republic'[9] we are told that everything has its own evil. Nor can anything be destroyed except by its specific evil. 'As mildew is of corn, and rot of timber, or rust of iron and steel, in everything, or in almost everything, there is an inherent evil and disease.' The evil of the soul is wickedness – 'unrighteousness, intemperance, cowardice, ignorance'. But the unjust and foolish do not perish through their injustice. Wickedness does not bring the soul to her death or separate her from the body. The opposite in fact happens, 'the injustice which murders others keeps the murderer alive'. The soul is not, therefore, destroyed by its proper evil, and it cannot be destroyed by anything else.

For, 'that the soul, or anything else which is not destroyed by an internal evil, can be destroyed by an external one, is not to be supposed'. This argument, if not as some suppose wholly verbal, leaves a great deal unexplained. It does nothing to show that the soul does, in fact, survive the dissolution of the body.

A somewhat more impressive argument is that which we find in the *Phaedrus*, whereby it is held that the soul must be the cause of all movement. It is itself self-moved. This seems at odds with our knowledge of the natural world, and it can only have significance when shifted from the sphere of particular causal efficacy to that of the contingent or dependent character of *all* finite things, including souls. Even then it is not of movement in the strict sense that we should speak, but of some original initiation or conferment of power, and, in taking this course, we retreat to the idea of an initial Unmoved Mover and are talking about God rather than man. As an anticipation of a famous argument for the existence of God, an argument which may contain an important insight even if it will not do as argument, the *Phaedrus* passage is not without significance. It does nothing to prove the indispensability of finite souls.

Another consideration which has prominence for Plato in these contexts is that of anamnesis or recollection, akin to the argument noted earlier in discussing reincarnation. How seriously Plato took this notion is not clear. In the *Meno* a slave-boy is induced by judicious questions and answers to provide the answer to a geometrical problem without any previous training. The boy appears to be producing the proof himself, and the suggestion here is that he has the understanding or knowledge already, only needing to be awakened by appropriate questions. Socrates himself concludes, for this reason, that the soul is immortal. But most of the time this particular thesis is presented in poetical terms and it is not clear how strictly we are to take it. The argument is certainly not a strong one. There are simpler accounts of the insights of the slave-boy, even if he proves to be a very precocious one, than pre-existence, and we have seen above that the sense of familiarity is not in itself enough to establish anything as bold and precise as reincarnation.

We cannot, therefore, deem Plato's arguments to be very impressive in themselves. Nor does it seem to me likely that any argument could show that any finite existent is inherently indestructible. But it is a notable fact that a thinker of Plato's range and imaginative insight should deem the soul to be of such worth that the destruction of it was unthinkable for him.

Aristotle's view is very different. For him the idea of the soul is more like the idea of an organising principle. In line with his distinction of form and matter there is accorded to us a vegetative soul at the plant level, a sensitive soul at the level of perception and a rational soul found only in man. Body and soul are not, on this view, separate entities. We are more in line here with the monistic view of persons which has played an important part in Western thought and is, as was noted, the most fashionable among philosophers today. The position remains, however, a little uncertain as far as Aristotle is concerned. For, at the upper level of form and matter he does recognise pure form, and he makes the principle of reason in us an exception to the correlativity of soul and body, in one place even speaking of the soul as the actuality of the body in the same way as the sailor is of the ship. For us to be actually intelligent there is also needed the active reason and this is sometimes spoken of as coming from without, and in the form of *Nous* it is regarded as self-existent substance. This seems clearly a departure from the standard Aristotelian line, but how much of a departure is not easy to determine. For Aristotle also thinks that actual reasoning, memory and affection belong to the composite whole of mind and body. This could be understood in terms of the idea of a self which is more than any of its particular states. But here we could also be reading more into Aristotle's thought than is warranted. As active principle Reason, for Aristotle, could be identified also with a divine activity which is identical in all men, and he has certainly been so understood by some of his followers. But this would pave the way for a very different understanding of immortality from that of any kind of personal survival.

God is, moreover, for Aristotle, pure form and exists in contemplation of his own perfection. He moves things only as the Unmoved Mover for whom it would be an indignity and imperfection to have concern for lesser beings. Here again we move from the context in which the preservation of the individual soul appears most plausible. We do not, therefore, find in Aristotle much support, far less explicit arguments, for the view of immortality which requires our continuation in being as the distinct persons we now know ourselves to be.

A notable modern philosopher who does provide an explicit argument for personal immortality is Kant. This argument is indeed a famous one, but, as in the case of Plato, it is more impressive as evidence of a profound conviction than as a water-tight argument – and that indeed is how he himself seems to regard it. Kant, as we have seen, thinks of the soul or self as the condition of our having knowledge of a world of objects, but it is not itself known as an object. For the same reason we cannot have knowledge, in the strict sense, of the eventual destiny of the soul. But here, as in the case of the existence of God, we can invoke the postulates of Practical Reason, to give us 'grounds for faith', not in the strictly religious sense of faith but as postulates of moral experience. The argument for immortality in this context centres on the fact that we are confronted by an absolute moral demand, a categorical imperative. It is a condition of a categorical imperative that we should be free to respond to it, and freedom is indeed listed as another postulate of Practical Reason. In spite of this, Kant concludes that we cannot render all that the ideal requires of us in the present existence, but, on the contrary, require an infinite time to strive after it. There are obvious difficulties in this argument. If it is held that, as sensitive beings having a desiring nature, we are inhibited from attaining the ideal, the inhibition seems absolute in a world where our desiring nature or empirical self is subject to strict determination as seems to be intended by Kant. The self as noumenon is in an entirely different realm, and it is hard to see what would limit its freedom to make a total response. Moving from the peculiar difficulties incidental to Kant's bifurcation of persons into noumena and phenomena, and looking at the argument in the context of common experience, it is hard to see in what sense we can be said to have any obligations which we are not expected to fulfil here and now.

The kind of obligations that Kant has in mind imply this, whether they be 'perfect' duties of truth-telling and keeping promises or 'imperfect' obligations to develop our talents, etc. There is, indeed, a sense in which an ideal is beyond our reach. There are things which I cannot achieve now, but may through cultivation of my gifts and character later. To achieve certain ends I also require the co-operation of others and social enactments. Some social ideals are, for this reason, bound to be ideals for the future. But no one is under a proper moral imperative to do more, in the furthering of various aims, than is within his reach at a particular time. Finally, even if there were a case for saying that the categorical imperative required an infinite time for us to strive after it, we would still need further assurance that this was, in fact, guaranteed; and so we would need to fall back on the third of Kant's postulates of reason, namely the existence of God, here again required in a somewhat artificial and incidental way as the guarantor of the ultimate union of happiness and virtue which we cannot, from the nature of moral obligation, set out to ensure for ourselves. Argumentation as strained as this is not likely to allay the restlessness and anxieties of those who 'at times are sober' and wonder what life may hold for them besides the fleeting and uncertain attainments of the present life.

This is where some will turn to the evidence from psychical research. I shall not try to assess that evidence further here. Some cautious and eminent investigators are convinced that contact is established in these ways with people who have died. If this confidence is justified the matter cannot fail to have the utmost importance. It is not, admittedly, the main or most direct way to break down the materialist presuppositions of much contemporary thought. That is much better accomplished by direct reflection on what we find to be the case in normal experience, and I have been much concerned with that undertaking earlier in this book. If, on the other hand, we can, with the aid of psychical research, provide strong or conclusive evidence of some kind of life after death, this should have momentous consequence and make a radical difference to the approach that many have to their problems here and now. It would open out hopes and perspectives which many do not entertain at all today, it would soften up a good deal of hard scepticism, and it may also tell us positively things we ought to heed about the life beyond and its bearing on our present life.

At the same time there seems to be a limit to what can be achieved in this way. A continuation of life in some form for what may be a limited duration is one thing, though there is no reason to suppose, from the present considerations, that it is bound to be limited in that way. But life eternal, in its fullness, is another matter. I am not thinking here of the rather tenuous and strange character of communications purporting to come from the dead. For H. H. Price may well be right here in ascribing that limitation to the difficulty of the communication and possible distortions. But the religious person has usually thought of life eternal as a particular quality of life and a very special relation to God or some spiritual reality. A good deal more seems to be involved in most religions than endlessness, and indeed endlessness seems to be itself transcended in some cases. But for this we must look to the religious context itself, and it is, moreover, in that context, rather than in general metaphysical arguments, that we can find the strongest and most enduring support for the view that this life is not all, however that is understood.

This does not mean that we forthwith dismiss the philosopher from the debate – far from it. We have already seen that, unless certain views about the nature of persons can be sustained and others rebutted, it is idle to embark on any consideration of life after death. Death is bound to be the end on many philosophical views, including those that are widely held today. But the philosopher may be called upon for a great deal more than this negative or propaedeutic work. He can help us to consider more positively what may be involved in some life hereafter, along the lines sketched

in earlier chapters of this book. That may not give us a
definitive view of what the future life may be like, but it may
rid us of certain misconceptions and eliminate difficulties
which might otherwise be daunting. It may also induce a
more realistic approach to the subject and put the prospects
held before us in a more exciting light. In these respects the
part which the philosopher has to play, in respect to the
hope of a 'life beyond', is a considerable one. Negatively
also he can help to clear out of the way irrelevant considerations or modes of argumentation which have little
substance and may discredit the enterprise from the start.

In addition, we must not forget the part which philosophy plays in the general sustaining of a religious view – or
in discrediting it as the case may be. Religion cannot thrive,
least of all today, at the level of blind or dogmatic affirmation. It must be reflective and submit to the scrutiny of
critical reason. That is certainly how it will emerge most
strongly, and I have been myself at pains in other writings
to indicate and defend the important place which philosophical reflection must play today in the general commendation of religion. This does not mean that we can
manufacture a religion out of philosophical reflections
alone. Certain insights of a distinctively religious kind are
needed, and elsewhere I have stressed the importance of
religious experience and distinctive religious occasions. But
reason has a central place in these, and the question of how
religious affirmations are to be understood and sustained is
a very proper concern of philosophers as is well borne out in
the attention which many philosophers are giving it today.
This book is not the place to pursue that theme further. The
main point at the moment is that it is in the rounded context of religious commitment, with whatever part reason
and philosophy play in this, that the hope of a life beyond
the present existence is most effectively and appropriately
sustained.

The way this hope is, in fact, sustained in different religions varies a great deal. In some we have extreme caution,
as in the religions which centre attention mainly on 'the
path' or the 'way', even when the goal is not defined in
terms of the way. Others are more explicit, and sometimes

religious expectations drop to the crudities of alleged celestial junketing or unrelieved indulgence in the pursuits to which we ought not to attach the greatest importance even in this life. To my mind the religions which bear most impressively on the issue of a 'life beyond' are the more overtly theistic ones, and among these the exhibition of the singular worth of individuals, not only in their relation with one another, but pre-eminently in fellowship with God, seems to be of prime importance. The Christian claims that the illimitable love of God is poured towards us and made evident in divine disclosures in history which are assimilated into profound individual and communal experience. Hebrew experience may not always have centred on the expectation of personal immortality, though it would be difficult to understand the profoundest moments of it, in prophecy, psalms or narrative without the regard of God for the individual which places us in some abiding relation with God. The temporal and national aspirations of the Hebrews gain their deepest significance in the context of God's seeking men out, in the innermost core of their own existence, as the object of his unlimited concern, and it would be very hard to understand this in the context of a total eclipse of the individual.

The central Christian affirmation is that the God who spoke to men at sundry times and in diverse manners has 'in these last days spoken unto us by his Son'. The Christian gospel is centred on the work and person of Christ. There are various ways in which this may be understood, and discussion of controversies on this subject would also take us far afield and require much space. But it seems difficult to give any fair account of the Christian gospel without regarding it as centred on a supreme intervention of God in the world to bring all men to right relation to himself. This concerns very closely the life we lead here and now; the Kingdom of God is 'within' us, and it is a great travesty of Christian truth to suppose that we should think of our salvation solely in terms of some destiny to be achieved later. It is a present reality, and the full realisation of this is essential to the appreciation of Christian claims and the impact they can have on our present attitudes. But however important this emphasis may be, and however necessary in the commendation of Christianity today, it would be odd, to say the least, if the peculiar relationship established between God and men in the coming of Christ were concerned wholly with the present life. It must surely be understood in the context of an abiding fellowship; the peculiarly personal character of the divine disclosure and intervention in Christ, the intimacy of the contexts in which Christ spoke and acted, seem to be violated in the assumption that it concerns solely the fleeting existence we have at present, the way we glow in the love of God for a brief interlude before we cease to be for ever. 'Behold', says the first Epistle of John, 'what manner of love the Father has bestowed upon us.' In this context it becomes imperative that we should love one another, and that is the central theme of the epistle. But by the same 'witness' and 'record' we know also 'that God hath given to us eternal life'. 'Beloved', then the apostle tells us, 'now we are the sons of God; and it doth not yet appear what we shall be: but we know that, when he shall appear, we shall be like him; for we shall see him as he is. And every man that hath this hope in him purifieth himself, even as he is pure.' This declaration is closely in line with the spirit and teaching of the Gospels. The appeal made to men is an immediate insistent one, but it is also the hope of life eternal. 'For God so loved the world, that he gave his only begotten son, that whosoever believeth in him should not perish, but have everlasting life.' The part which the resurrection of Jesus plays in this assurance is also a central one for most Christians, but the way this is to be understood is also a topic in itself. The most that I will add here is that the resurrection narratives must be understood in the full context of the Christian witness as found in the Gospels as a whole. In that context the promise that, as Christ is risen, we shall be raised up with him can be properly apprehended.

In this there are two excesses to be avoided. On the one hand, we must be careful not to take metaphorical utterances out of their context and in too literal a sense. On the other hand, we must not lapse into the attenuation which deprives the expectation of the life everlasting in sanctified fellowship with a risen Lord of all its proper significance. To work out the implications of this and consider closely how the Christian promises must be understood is a task in itself and it would take us well beyond the scope of this book. My aim has been a modest one of indicating how we must think of persons in the context that is most relevant to Christian and related affirmations of a positive expectation of a life beyond the grave. We shall, I hope, be able to avoid the excesses noted earlier in this passage if we think of the problem along the lines indicated in this book. I hope we shall also find the way open for cautious speculation which will have as one of its consequences a much deeper appreciation of the significance of life as we live it now, and the context in which our major present concerns can be properly viewed – 'While we look not at the things which are seen, but at the things which are not seen; for the things which are seen are temporal; but the things which are not seen are eternal.'

Notes

CHAPTER 1

1. How far the historical Socrates, by contrast with Plato, held such a view is still in dispute among scholars. Some maintain that Socrates himself had an agnostic attitude on life after death.
2. ' "Well," said I, "Mr Hume, I hope to triumph over you in a future state; and remember you are not to pretend that you was joking with all this infidelity." "No, no", said he, "but I shall have been so long there before you come that it will be nothing new." '
3. Op. cit., p.430.

CHAPTER 2

1. Most of all in the 'Republic'. In the 'Phaedo' more stress is laid on the dangers of 'excessive tendance of the body'.
2. 'Republic', bk. x, 611.
3. 'Nature, Man and God', Lectures III and IV.
4. It is a sad reflection on the biased and hasty character of much recent thought that these words of Descartes are often cited as if Descartes himself were using them in the sense that the mind was in this way 'in' the body, when in fact he was expressly warning us not to think in that way or misinterpret him.
5. 'Phaedo', 115 (Jowett's translation).

CHAPTER 3

1. 'The comparison of the theatre must not mislead us. They are the successive perceptions only, that constitute the

mind; nor have we the most distant notion of the place, where these scenes are represented, or of the materials of which it is compos'd.' Hume's 'Treatise', Selby Bigge, 2nd ed., p. 253.

2. 'A Treatise of Human Nature', bk. I, pt. 4, sec. 6.

3. Another well-known term which Kant uses here is *noumenon, noumena* being contrasted with *phenomena* – things as they appear to us.

4. On the very difficult question of the relation, for Kant, of the self as subject to the self as a thing in itself, Dr A. C. Ewing has the following comment: 'But the difficulty as to what it is precisely that I, on Kant's view, know in knowing that I think cannot be said to be removed. In §25 he says that I thus know that I am, but not what I am. This would suggest that in being aware of the transcendental unity of apperception I am conscious that there is a real (noumenal) self though I can never attain any knowledge of its nature. On the other hand, all or almost all the other passages which deal with the transcendental unity of apperception imply that it is only a unity of experience and not a self independent of and, so to speak, behind all experience like the thing-in-itself. In that case we must distinguish three aspects of the self – the phenomenal self, the noumenal self and the transcendental unity of apperception. The third is not an existent but a form to which all experience is subject. Kant, however, no doubt believed, though he did not claim to *know*, that this form could only be imposed by a noumenal self and presupposed the existence of the latter.' 'A Short Commentary on Kant's Critique of Pure Reason', pp. 126–7.

5. James Ward, 'Psychological Principles', p. 381.

6. Op. cit., p. 378.

7. Op. cit., p. 381. On this Ward and Tennant are in close agreement. Tennant wrote: 'The permanent ego or the soul, is not intuited, in the sense of being immediately apprehended, as is a sense-datum, but reflectively: self-consciousness is mediated partly by cognition of external objects, and not by introspection alone. On the other hand, the data of sensory individual experience only yield

knowledge of the world when overlaid by categories which are ultimately derived from the soul itself, and which owe their conceptual elaboration to communication with other selves. Knowledge of the self and knowledge of the world are interdependent from the first stages which we can trace and grow *pari passu*' 'Philosophical Theology', vol. II, p. 252.

8. Op. cit., p. 379.

CHAPTER 4

1. 'The Concept of Mind', p. 12.
2. 'The Problems of Perception', p. 185
3. 'Philosophical Theology', vol. II, p. 252.
4. 'The Concept of Mind', p. 15.
5. It could be argued, of course, that we need not, even in the absence of a distinct impact of mind on body, hold to a strict physical determination of bodily states, Not all materialists have been determinists. But the coincidence of any break in the causal continuity of physical processes with purposing which does not bring about such a break, would indeed be remarkable.
6. 'Body and Mind', p. 54.
7. 'The Problems of Perception', chap. VII.

CHAPTER 5

1. 'Treatise', bk. I, pt. 4, sect. 6.
2. Book II, chap. 1.
3. Cf. Shoemaker, op. cit., pp. 40 and 75.
4. 'Personal Identity and Individuation', 'Proceedings of the Aristotelian Society', 1956–57.
5. Op. cit., p. 223.
6. Op. cit., p. 190.
7. 'The Elusive Mind', chap. X.

8. 'Essay concerning Human Understanding', bk. ii, chap. 27.
9. 'The Elusive Mind', pp. 217–18.
10. 'Self-knowledge and Self-identity', p. 202.

CHAPTER 7

1. Muhammad did not presumably write anything either but his words were taken down at the time by those who heard what he says in the Qur'an.
2. See his 'Rational Grounds of Belief in God' in his 'Statement and Inference', vol. ii.
3. 'The Elusive Mind', chap. xiii.
4. On this cf. a fascinating article by H. H. Price in 'Philosophy' for October 1938, 'Our Evidence for the Existence of other Minds'.
5. 'The Concept of a Person', p. 109.

CHAPTER 8

1. 'The Founder of Christianity', p. 42.
2. 'Public and Private Space', 'Proceedings of the Aristotelian Society', 1952.
3. Norman Malcolm, 'Dreaming'. For discussion of this book see my own L. T. Hobhouse Memorial Lecture, 'Dreaming and Experience', reproduced in chap. vi of my 'The Elusive Mind'.
4. 'Brain and Mind', p. 5.
5. 'Republic', 574.
6. 'Theology Today', April 1960.
7. Luke 16, 26.
8. J. J. Clarke, 'Sophia'.

CHAPTER 9

1. 'Individuals', p. 124.

2. Op. cit., p. 131.
3. Op. cit., p. 86.
4. Op. cit., p. 85.
5. Op. cit., p. 83.
6. Op. cit., p. 132.
7. 'Introduction to the Qur'an', p. 29.

CHAPTER 10

1. 'Ethics', pt. v, xxiii.
2. 'The Idea of God', p. 269.
3. 'The Elusive Mind', p. 308.
4. Op. cit., p. 58
5. Op. cit., p. 58.
6. Op. cit., p. 58.
7. Op. cit., p. 63; cf. above, Chapter 5.
8. Op. cit., p. 67.
9. Op. cit., p. 66.
10. Op. cit., p. 68.

CHAPTER 11

1. Brain and Mind, p. 1.
2. Ibid.
3. 'Laws', 959.
4. 'Sophist', 248e.
5. 'The Idea of Immortality', p. 59.
6. 'Apology', 30.
7. 'Laws', 959.
8. Above, p. 17.
9. Pp. 608 – 11.

Bibliography

ATTITUDES TO DEATH

Plato, 'The Apology', 'Phaedo'.

√ S. Findlay, 'Immortal Longings' (Gollancz, 1961).

R. Aldwinkle, 'Death in the Secular City' (Allen & Unwin, 1972).

A. Toynbee *et al.*, 'Man's Concern with Death' (Hodder & Stoughton, 1968).

C. F. Mooney (ed.), 'The Presence and Absence of God' (Fordham University Press, 1969). See especially the contribution by L. F. Gilbey.

√P. J. Saher, 'Happiness and Immortality' (Allen & Unwin, 1970).

√A. Farrer, 'Love Almighty and Ills Unlimited' (Collins, 1962).

C. A. Campbell, 'On Selfhood and Godhood', Lec. xiii and xiv (Allen & Unwin, 1957).

W. Temple, 'Nature, Man and God', Lec. xviii (Macmillan, 1935).

L. Harold DeWolf, 'A Theology of the Living Church' (Harper, 1953) chapters 26 and 27.

√J. Piefer, 'Death and Immortality' (Burns & Oates, 1969).

MIND AND BODY

Historical and Selected Reading

A. Flew (ed.), 'Body, Mind and Death' (Collier-Macmillan Series, 1964).

G. N. A. Vesey, 'Body and Mind' (Allen & Unwin, 1964).

V. C. Chappell (ed.), 'The Philosophy of Mind' (Prentice-Hall Inc., 1962).

S. Hook (ed.), 'Dimensions of Mind' (Collier Books, New York, 1961). A symposium.

C. A. Van Peursen, 'Body, Soul, Spirit', translated by H. H. Hoskins (Oxford University Press, 1966).

Keith Campbell, 'Body and Mind' (Macmillan, 1970).

General

J. Ward, 'Psychological Principles' (Cambridge, 1918).

C. D. Broad, 'The Mind and Its Place in Nature' (Routledge & Kegan Paul, 1925).

G. F. Stout, 'Mind and Matter' (1931).

C. Sherrington, 'Man on His Nature'

R. M. Zaner, 'The Problems of Embodiment' (Martinus Nighoff, The Hague, 1964).

G. N. A. Vesey (ed.), 'The Human Agent', Royal Institute of Philosophy Lectures, vol. I (Macmillan, 1965).

N. Hartmann, 'Ethics', vol. III (Allen & Unwin, 1932).

Recent Controversy – Books

This list starts with books opposed to dualism and proceeds to works which favour it.

G. Ryle, 'The Concept of Mind' (Hutchinson, 1947).

C. V. Borst (ed.), 'The Mind–Brain Identity Theory' (Macmillan, 1970).

J. J. C. Smart, 'Philosophy and Scientific Realism' (Routledge & Kegan Paul, 1963).

S. Hampshire, 'Thought and Action' (Chatto & Windus, 1959).

H. Feigl, 'Minnesota Studies in the Philosophy of Science', vol. II (1957).

A. J. Ayer, 'The Concept of a Person' (1963).

——'The Problem of Knowledge' (Pelican, 1956). 'Philosophical Essays' (1954).

N. Malcolm, 'Dreaming' (Routledge & Kegan Paul, 1959).

J. Passmore, 'Philosophical Reasoning' (Duckworth, 1961).

P. Geach, 'Mental Acts' (Routledge & Kegan Paul, 1957).

D. M. Armstrong, 'Bodily Sensations' (Routledge & Kegan Paul, 1962).

G. N. A. Vesey, 'The Embodied Mind' (Allen & Unwin, 1965).

P. Strawson, 'Individuals' (Methuen, 1959).

——'The Bounds of Sense' (Methuen, 1966).

S. Coval, 'Scepticism and the First Person' (Methuen, 1966).

H. D. Lewis (ed.), 'Clarity is Not Enough' (Allen & Unwin, 1963).

J. R. Smythies, 'Brain and Mind' (Routledge & Kegan Paul, 1965).

D. Browning, 'Act and Agent' (University of Miami Press, 1964).

W. R. Brain, 'Mind, Perception and Science' (Blackwell, 1951).

W. Kneale, 'On Having a Mind' (Cambridge University Press, 1962).

C. A. Campbell, 'On Selfhood and Godhood' (Allen & Unwin, 1957).

A. C. Ewing, 'Non-Linguistic Philosophy' (Allen & Unwin, 1968).

J. Beloff, 'The Existence of Mind' (Macgibbon & Kee, 1962).

Recent Controversy – Articles

J. Shaffer, 'The Mind–Body Problem', in 'The Encyclopedia of Philosophy', ed. P. Edwards, vol. v.

M. Kneale, 'What is the Mind–Body Problem?', in 'Proceedings of the Aristotelian Society', vol. l.

J. O. Wisdom, 'Some Main Mind–Body Problems', in 'Proceedings of the Aristotelian Society', vol. lx.

M. Scriven, 'The Mechanical Concept of Mind', in 'Mind' (1953).

H. G. Alexander, 'Paying Heed', in 'Mind' (1953).

G. W. Pilkington and W. D. Glagow, 'On the Soul', in 'Mind', vol. lxviii.

J. Margolis, 'I Exist', in 'Mind', vol. lxxiii.

A. R. Louch, 'Privileged Access', in 'Mind', vol. lxxiv.

S. Candlish, 'Mind, Brain and Identity', in 'Mind', vol. lxxix.

T. R. Miles, 'The "Mental–Physical" Dichotomy', in 'Proceedings of the Aristotelian Society', vol. LXIV.

J. J. C. Smart, 'Sensations and Brain Processes', in 'The Philosophical Review', vol. LXVIII.

D. C. Long, 'The Philosophical Concept of a Human Body', in 'The Philosophical Review', vol. LXXIV.

N. Malcolm, 'Descartes: Proof That His Essence is Thinking', in 'The Philosophical Review', vol. LXXIV.

J. Shaffer, 'Persons and Their Bodies', in 'The Philosophical Review', vol. LXXV.

SELF-IDENTITY

This is considered in many of the works already listed. Note, in addition, the following:

T. Penelhum, 'Personal Identity', in 'Encyclopedia of Philosophy', ed. P. Edwards, vol. 6.

J. Laird, 'The Problem of the Self' (Macmillan, 1917).

S. Shoemaker, 'Self-Knowledge and Self-Identity' (Cornell University Press, 1963).

B. A. Williams, 'Personal Identity and Individuation' in 'Proceedings of the Aristotelian Society', vol. LVII.

B. Williams, 'The Self and the Future', in 'The Philosophical Review', vol. LXXIX.

D. Parfit, 'Personal Identity', in 'The Philosophical Review', vol. LXXX.

J. O. Nelson, 'The Validation of Memory and Our Conception of a Past', in 'The Philosophical Review', vol. LXXII.

S. Shoemaker, 'Persons and Their Pasts', in 'American Philosophical Quarterly', vol. 7, no. 4.

J. M. Shorter, 'Personal Identity', in 'Proceedings of the Aristotelian Society', vols. LXX – LXXI.

I. T. Ramsey, 'The Systematic Elusiveness of "I" ', in 'The Philosophical Quarterly', vol. 5.

OTHER MINDS

H. H. Price, 'The Evidence for the Existence of Other Minds', in 'Philosophy' (October 1938).

J. Wisdom, 'Other Minds' (Oxford, 1956).

N. Malcolm, 'Knowledge of Other Minds', in 'Journal of Philosophy', vol. 55.

J. M. Shorter, 'Other Minds', in 'Encyclopedia of Philosophy', ed. P. Edwards, vol. 6.

J. F. Thomson, 'The Argument from Analogy and Our Knowledge of Other Minds', in 'Mind', vol. LX.

H. Dingle, 'Solipsism and Related Matters', in 'Mind', vol. LXIV.

A. Plantinga, 'God and Other Minds' (Cornell University Press, 1967).

B. Aune, 'The Problem of Other Minds', in 'The Philosophical Review', vol. LXX.

SURVIVAL AND IMMORTALITY

S. H. Mellone, 'Immortality', in 'Encyclopaedia of Religion and Ethics', ed. J. Hastings, vol. VII.

A. Flew, 'Immortality', in 'Encyclopedia of Philosophy', ed. P. Edwards, vol. 4.

Various authors, 'The Soul', in 'Encyclopaedia of Religion and Ethics', ed. J. Hastings, vol. XI.

Joseph Butler, 'Dissertation I, of Personal Identity'.

A. S. Pringle-Pattison, 'The Idea of Immortality' (Oxford Press, 1922).

T. Penelhum, 'Survival and Disembodied Existence' (Routledge & Kegan Paul, 1970).

J. A. Harvie, 'The Immortality of the Soul', in 'Religious Studies', vol. 5, no. 2.

I. T. Ramsey, 'Freedom and Immortality' (S. C. M. Press, 1960).

G. Parrinder, 'Avatar and Incarnation' (Faber & Faber, 1970).

C. Green, 'Out-of-the-Body Experience' (Oxford, 1968).

C. D. Broad, 'Lectures on Psychical Research' (Routledge & Kegan Paul, 1962).

I. Stevenson, 'Twenty Cases Suggestive of Reincarnation' (American Society for Psychical Research, 1966).

M. Bernstein, 'The Search for Bridey Murphy' (Doubleday, 1956).

J. Knox, Jr., 'Can the Self Survive the Death of Its Mind?', in 'Religious Studies', vol. 5, no. 1.

S. R. Sutherland, 'Immortality and Resurrection', in 'Religious Studies', vol. 3.

H. H. Price, 'The Problem of Life After Death', in 'Religious Studies', vol. 3.

John Baillie, 'And the Life Everlasting' (OUP, 1934).

A. E. Taylor, 'The Christian Hope of Immortality' (Geoffrey Bles, The Centenary Press, 1946).

J. N. D. Kelly, 'Early Christian Doctrines', part 4 (Macmillan, 1960).

M. E. Dahl, 'The Resurrection of the Body' (S. C. M. Press, 1962).

K. Stendhal, 'Immortality and Resurrection' (New York: Macmillan, 1965).

Index of Proper Names

Index of Subjects